STAFFORDSHIRE MURDERS

ALAN HAYHURST

First published in the United Kingdom in 2008 by
The History Press
The Mill, Brimscombe Port,
Stroud, Gloucestershire, GL5 2QG
www.thehistorypress.co.uk

Reprinted 2009

British Library Cataloguing in Publication Data
A catalogue record for this book is available from the British Library.

ISBN 978 0 7509 4706 0

Typesetting and origination by
The History Press.
Printed and bound in England.

CONTENTS

ACKNOWLEDGEMENTS

The author would like to thank the staff of the National Archives at Kew and especially Carole-Ann Montgomery, the Freedom of Information Assessor, who worked hard to produce a number of files to which access had formerly been denied; Rebecca Jackson and the staff at Staffordshire Record Office; the William Salt Library, Stafford; Stoke-on-Trent City Archives, Hanley; Leon Jeavons and Yvonne Cooper at the Museum of Cannock Chase, Hednesford, who were able to provide much helpful information and a copy of a rare postcard; Paul Bedford, for his help with the Gaskin case; Brian and Joan Braybrooke for bringing to my attention the mysterious shooting at Talke; Richard Wilcox for the loan of several books; Bill Eddisbury, who was a mine of information on the Trent & Mersey Canal system; Alan and Marie Elmer, booksellers extraordinaire; Stewart Evans; Matilda Pearce, Simon Fletcher and the team at Sutton Publishing; *Midland Ancestor*, the magazine of the Birmingham & Midland Society for Genealogy and Heraldry; Alan Walker, curator of the Staffordshire Police Museum (now sadly closed); and numerous other people who have been helpful in one way or another. Finally my thanks, as usual, to my wife, without whose forbearance and countless cups of coffee this volume would never have seen the light of day.

INTRODUCTION

For most people, until comparatively recently, life in Staffordshire was harsh. Employment was to be found mainly in agriculture, the pottery industry and the mines, and many found that the antidote to long working hours and poor pay was only too often to be found in the bottle. Later on, working conditions improved, although if anything the dreadfulness of the murders in the county increased; some of them pointless, as in the killing of Donald Lainton by Arthur Cross, and others still showing the age-old ingredients of revenge and greed, as demonstrated so well by the horrendous killing of Alice Maud Wiltshaw by Leslie Green.

Perhaps man has always had an aggressive, not to say evil, side to him – all the murderers in this book are male and almost all the victims are female – but what can be said is that the death penalty, exacted upon most of the killers whose stories are recounted here, was never a deterrent. Murders tend to be a spur of the moment matter and there is often little or no time to consider the outcome of one's actions. The sad tales of baby-killer Frederick Edge and the surely wronged Henry Thomas Gaskin demonstrate this exactly.

The author has consulted newspapers of the time and files in the appropriate Record Offices, as well as other contemporaneous accounts contained in letters and diaries, and has spoken to people who have either memories or documentary evidence of the crimes concerned. Where speech is reported, effort has been made to ensure that the words are as exact as can be, many of them extracted from verbatim reports published at the time. During researches at the National Archives, Kew, I came across no fewer than ten files which were closed to the public for periods of up to 100 years from the time of the event; but using the Freedom of Information Act 2000, I was able to gain access to no less than nine of them, although the photographs in one case were denied to me, as they were 'likely to endanger the physical or mental health or safety of an individual.' The tenth file met with a blank refusal.

In some cases, it was difficult to tell why a particular file should ever have been embargoed (one file merely contained a transcript of the trial), and the photographs that I was allowed to see did not contain anything that is not freely available on television any night of the week, but at least the majority of the papers I asked for were produced and there are therefore some details of the particular crimes in this book which will not have been in the public domain before.

Finally, when researching a book dealing with a particular county, one comes across the problem that boundaries, for one reason or another, do alter over the years. For instance, Walsall is now in the county of West Midlands whereas formerly it was in Staffordshire. The final story, dealing with the Cannock Chase murders, inevitably has to include details of certain actions in what is now classified as the West Midlands, but I hope that this will not detract from what is still essentially a Staffordshire murder.

1

THE BLOODY STEPS MURDER

Colwich, 1839

Christina Collins was about 37 years of age, diminutive in size although not unattractive and had been twice married; a not unusual state of affairs in the days when a widow's lot was much harder than it is today, both financially and socially. She was the daughter of a middle-class Nottingham inventor, who had had some minor successes with patents involving the lace industry, and it was rumoured that she had some connections with the Covent Garden Theatre in London. Her first husband was one Thomas Ingleby, a Scotsman, who travelled the country exhibiting his conjuring skills in the music halls.

Being anything but a shrinking violet, Ingleby boasted on his handbills – which he gave out to whoever would deign to read them – that he was the 'Emperor of all Conjurers,' but his conjuring skills did not translate into money, for when he died in Ireland in 1832 he left his wife with little or nothing. Christina, from sheer force of necessity, looked around for another husband and was fortunate to attract Robert Collins, who worked with horses and with whom she was soon deeply in love; although it was not until 1838 that they married and went to Liverpool, looking for work. Despite trying his best, Collins found it impossible to get employment in the north and reluctantly decided that he must seek his fortune in London, leaving his newly-wed wife alone in Liverpool, where she found employment as a dressmaker, with Mrs Grice of 3 Crosshall Street.

Robert quickly found work in London and settled into lodgings at 10 Edgware Road and Christina was overjoyed when she received a letter from him asking her to join him and enclosing a golden guinea to cover the cost of the journey. This was more than likely the largest sum of money that Christina had ever had at one time but even that was insufficient to enable her to travel in reasonable comfort by coach. All she could afford was a passage on a narrow boat via the canal system, a journey that would be slow, with little in the way of comforts, but this meant nothing to Christina as she thought of the day when she and her beloved Robert would be reunited.

On 15 June 1839, Christina left Liverpool and travelled by barge to Preston Brook, on the Trent & Mersey Canal, to join one of Messrs Pickford's boats, the *Staffordshire Knot*, which was due to sail via Stoke-on-Trent, Rugeley, Fradley Junction and thence by Coventry to London. Christina was wearing a dark-coloured gown, a fawn-coloured handkerchief over her neck, and a figured blue silk bonnet with a light ribbon. Everything else that she owned was packed into two small cases.

The crew of the boat consisted of James Owen, the captain, assisted by two boatmen, George Thomas, alias Dobell, who had been with Pickford's for seven years and came from Westborne, and William Ellis, alias Lambert, from Brinklow, near Rugby, who had only been with the boat for a few weeks. There was also a cabin boy, William Muston (this lad's name was also given as Musson). It is highly unlikely that any of the crew, with the possible exception of Owen, could read or write, which might excuse the confusion of names.

The genteel Christina must have been somewhat taken aback at the first sight of this ruffianly crew, with whom she would perforce have to share the restricted accommodation that the barge offered for more than a week, and her fears increased when she noticed that the boat was stopping at regular intervals along the way while the crew, including young Muston, kept up their strength and their spirits by drinking their fill of the local ale. James Owen downed seven pints when the boat stopped at Stoke wharf – where Christina was seen by George Neville, one of Pickford's clerks, sitting in the boat reading a novel – and he carried a further gallon to the boat to keep them going until the next stop at Barlaston, conveniently near to the Plume of Feathers public house. While the boat stopped there, Christina went into the Pickford's office, where the clerk, thinking she looked rather tired, allowed her to doze fitfully until cries from outside told them that the narrow boat was ready to move on.

By the time they reached Walton, near Stone, the situation had deteriorated and Christina was now fearful for her safety. She told Hugh Cordwell, the canal clerk, that she was afraid that the crew would 'meddle with her' in their present drunken state, and, rather unhelpfully, Cordwell advised her that if they did, she must report them at the journey's end! His strictures were interrupted by a loud crash as the boat rammed the lock gates, followed by a torrent of abusive language from the captain. The air turned even bluer when Cordwell remonstrated with James Owen, but eventually things were sorted out and the boat proceeded. While all this was going on, Christina again stepped off the boat and proceeded to walk along the towpath. She walked with such determination that she soon outstripped the boat and Catherine Tansley, the wife of the lockkeeper at Aston, recalled seeing her there at about 8.30 p.m. waiting for the boat to catch up. While she sat, she passed the time by sharpening a penknife on the stone steps.

The much-altered Plume of Feathers public house, 2007. One of several 'refuelling' stops for the crew of the Staffordshire Knot. *(Author's collection)*

On arrival at the lock, one of the men on the boat pointed to Christina and shouted, 'Curse her eyes – I wish she was in hell flames,' which, hardly surprisingly, made the poor woman burst into tears. Catherine Tansley also maintained that two of the men on the boat had been quarrelling and George Thomas had said that he would not work the boat any longer 'If she were allowed to be in the cabin' – instead of in the space reserved for passengers. The captain told him to take no notice, but this did not seem to satisfy Thomas, who said that if the captain would pay him the 10s wages he was due, he would leave the boat immediately. Why Thomas was so concerned about Christina being in the cabin with them was never explained.

The crew were evidently still very much inebriated but Christina had little choice but to rejoin the boat as it set off along the canal towards Hoo Mill lock, where the lockkeeper's wife, Ann Mills, later recollected that she was awakened at about midnight that night by a woman's cry, which caused her to get up, open the window and look out. A woman was on the deck of a narrow boat, crying quietly to herself, although she did not speak. 'What's up?' cried Ann, and one of the boatmen shouted that they had 'Been in the canal,' at which the woman stepped off the boat and asked for her shoes, which she bent down to put on. Shortly afterwards, the lockkeeper's wife heard the woman say to one of the men on the boat, 'Don't attempt me – I'll not go down.'

Hoo Mill lock, where the lockkeeper's wife was awakened by Christina Collins' cries.
(Author's collection)

While the boat was in the lock, Ann Mills asked one of the boatmen who the woman was and received the reply that she was a passenger and that she had her husband with her. This quietened Ann's fears somewhat and eventually the boat went on its way.

At about 5 o'clock on Monday morning, Thomas Grant, a boatman, was approaching Brindley Bank, near Rugeley, when he saw something in the water. On closer inspection it turned out to be the body of a woman. She was dressed in a blue spotted gown and blue stockings, but without either bonnet or shoes. She was quite dead and although he looked, Grant saw neither footmarks on the canal bank nor any sign of how the woman had got into the water. Manoeuvring his boat skilfully, he pushed the body into the canal side and wharfinger John Johnson dragged the still warm body out of the water. Under the instructions of the parish constable, the body was carried, with some difficulty, up the wooden steps leading to the top of the steep bank and from there was eventually deposited at the Talbot Inn, Rugeley, where the inquest was to take place.

An hour later, Owen's boat passed through King's Bromley and was approaching Woodend lock, when Owen, clearly in a confused state, spoke to the lockkeeper's wife and said to her, 'I doubt we have had a passenger drowned.' When she enquired where, Owen said that he did not know. In

The Trent & Mersey Canal near Rugeley, where Christina Collins' body was found. (Author's collection)

answer to further questions, Owen, trembling visibly, said that the woman had been in the canal and that he had pulled her out and put her in the cabin. He said that she had seemed deranged and the only words he could make any sense out of were 'Collins, Collins.'

A little later on, Owen's boat reached Fradley Junction, where they were due to turn into the Coventry Canal. While they were changing horses, Owen told Charles Robotham, the Pickford's clerk, that he had had a passenger on board and that she had drowned herself. She had already attempted this once before, shouting all the while 'Collins, Collins,' which he believed was the name of her husband, and he had pulled her out. When asked by the shocked Robotham why he had allowed the woman to make a second attempt at drowning, he simply replied that he thought the woman was off her head. Owen asked Robotham if he would take the woman's things off the boat, but was interrupted by George Thomas, who said that the woman would follow them presently, which seemingly implied that she was still alive.

Meanwhile, William Harrison, the police constable at Fazeley, had been alerted by Charles Robotham of the strange goings-on taking place along the towpath, and was waiting for Owen's boat when it arrived. Before he could utter a word, one of the boatman burst out vehemently, 'Damn and blast the woman. What do I know about her? If she had a mind to drown herself, she might!' It was clear to PC Harrison that the crew, with the exception of the boy Muston, were inebriated. He quickly summoned assistance and the men, still cursing and swearing, were handcuffed and taken to the police station, where they were questioned further. Owen said that the woman had jumped out of the boat and that he had tried to hold on to her. 'In that case,' said PC Harrison, 'Why did you let her go?' to which Owen had no coherent reply. 'She was a little, fierce-talking woman,' he said, 'And I thought she was not quite right.'

In the cabin, PC Harrison found a bonnet, which was crushed; a pair of shoes tied together, a pair of clogs and an apron. Owen said that the apron belonged to his wife, but the rest were his passenger's. A short time before, PC Harrison discovered that the boy, Muston, had managed to slip his handcuffs, but before he could make off he was promptly locked safely in another room. Muston now said that he wished to be examined and after being shown the body, he identified it as the passenger who had come on board at Preston Brook, bound for London. 'She did not ride in the part of the boat usually set aside for passengers, but was in the cabin most of the way,' he told the policeman.

An inquest was convened at the Talbot Inn, Rugeley, before the coroner, Robert Fowke, and what was described in the *Staffordshire Advertiser* as a 'very respectable jury.'

According to Muston, who insisted on being heard, the woman had accompanied the three men to the public house when the boat stopped at Stoke Wharf, leaving him behind. They were gone for some time but when they returned, another woman, whom Muston thought was the ostler's wife, hitched a ride on the boat and stayed with their passenger for about three miles, before disembarking. After that, he went to sleep and did not wake up until the boat reached Colwich. According to the young lad, Owen and Christina were in the same bed, the captain being undressed, although the woman had all her clothes on. The woman then got off the boat and went towards the hedge, presumably to relieve herself, and that was the last time he saw her alive.

Arriving at Brindley Bank, near the aqueduct, it occurred to Muston to ask where the woman was. Someone, he said, suggested that she had fallen overboard and Owen, together with Thomas, went back to search for her. Dawn was breaking as Muston brought the boat to Rugeley wharf, where he fastened it up until the two men came back with the news that they had seen nothing of the missing woman.

The young lad may well have been frightened for his life when he was arrested, but his evidence seems to have been a pack of lies. He claimed that the woman had never been in the water at any time, that he had seen no clothes drying and that the men were sober. This last statement was palpably untrue, given the considerable amount of ale that the crew had consumed since they set off from Preston Brook, and he also denied that Christina had ever cried out 'Collins, Collins.'

George Thomas was questioned next and confirmed Muston's statement about the captain and Christina being in the same bed together, but denied that she had got off the boat at Colwich lock. He claimed that he fell asleep and was woken by Owen near Brindley Bank and told that the woman had disappeared. The two men went back along the towpath until Thomas decided that he would go no further. No explanation was given for this decision. The deceased had told him that she was a married woman and he had also heard her call out 'Collins' on several occasions.

William Ellis repeated most of Thomas's story but claimed that Christina and the captain were 'uncommonly united.' Again, this seems to fly in the face of what we know about the woman and her relationship with the crew.

James Owen was then taken to see the body of the deceased woman, which he formally identified and afterwards answered a series of questions, broadly along the lines of the replies given by Thomas and Ellis. He gave his answers slowly, with much caution, and said that all three men had drunk a quantity of porter at a beer shop in Stoke (he said three quarts and a pint, although Ellis insisted that it was no more than two quarts). All three men stoutly denied that the woman had consumed any alcohol with them.

He went on to say that he had gone to bed at Aston lock and had awoken at Haywood lock and found the woman in the cabin, crying. He believed at that time that Thomas had been interfering with her and in reply to his question, she said 'O captain, O my Collins, I will drown myself before I get to London.' When he tried to question her further, the woman burst into further sobbing and waved him away. Owen also claimed that he had borrowed 6s from the boy Muston, with the intention of paying Thomas off, but approaching Colwich lock, the spat between them seemed to have calmed down and he and Thomas were again working the boat together. By the time they got to Colwich, he did not know where the woman was, being too busy with the boat, and claimed that he had pulled her out of the water sometime earlier. However, she then insisted on climbing up on to the cabin top and the last he saw of her alive, she was standing on the towpath at Colwich. He thought that Christina must have got back on the boat before they moved off and had thrown herself into the water sometime before they reached Rugeley.

Owen also claimed that the other two men were in liquor and when asked how much, he replied, 'I durst not say how much lest they should dash my brains out!'

Neither the coroner nor anyone else commented on the fact that the canal was only 3ft 6in deep along that section, so that if she had fallen into the water while conscious, Christina might easily have waded to the canal bank and would have been unlikely to drown.

Mr Samuel Barnett, a local surgeon, made a post-mortem examination of the body and could find little in the way of wounds, apart from two small external bruises, which he thought of no consequence. He was of the opinion that Christina Collins had died by suffocation, caused by drowning, and further examination showed that no improper connection had taken place.

It was nearly eleven o'clock in the evening when the examination finished and the coroner adjourned the inquest until the following Monday morning at ten o'clock, ordering that the prisoners should all be kept separately and not be allowed to communicate with one another.

Upon resumption, and after further questioning of James Owen and his two colleagues, during which Owen tried to imply that he was sober, whereas Ellis and Thomas were heavily in drink at the time of Christina's death, the jury gave a 'Guilty' verdict and the three men were charged with the murder of Christina Collins, the boy Muston being allowed to go free.

At the subsequent trial, in front of Mr Justice Williams, which commenced at Stafford on 24 July 1839, Owen, Thomas and Ellis were put up on four separate counts; the first charged them with the wilful murder of Christina Collins by throwing her into the canal, the second was an accusation of rape on the woman, another indictment charged them with common assault and the fourth with stealing certain articles, the property of the husband of the deceased, to which all three accused pleaded not guilty. The boy Muston, it was announced, although originally charged with the others, would now appear as a witness for the Crown. Appearing for the prosecution at Stafford Crown Court were Sergeant Ludlow and Mr F.V. Lee, and for the accused were Mr Godson (for Owen), Mr Yardley (for Thomas) and Mr Beadon (for Ellis).

Sergeant Ludlow opened the proceedings by announcing that he would first move the charge of rape and it was his intention not to offer any evidence against James Owen, as he was willing to act as a witness for the Crown. Mr Godson immediately rose and told the judge that this course of action was being taken without Owen's consent. Mr Yardley and Mr Beadon, on hearing this surprising news, protested that this would greatly hamper them in their defence of the other two men and the discussion among learned counsel became rather heated, so much so that the judge intervened, saying that as the case was one of supreme importance, he would take the advice of his learned brother Mr Baron Alderson, who was trying a case in another court. He therefore suspended the hearing and when he returned, whatever doubts he had previously entertained appeared to have evaporated and he rather belligerently announced that there was now very little doubt in his mind as to the proper course to be taken in this case. He had known instances, not once, but hundreds of times, when the court had allowed counsel for the prosecution to withhold evidence against one of the accused parties so that they might give evidence on behalf of the Crown.

Sergeant Ludlow then opened his case, which he said was a very important one, involving as it did the life or death of the prisoners. He then proceeded to give a short résumé of the life of Christina Collins and her intention of travelling to London aboard the *Staffordshire Knot*. The evidence would show, he told the court, that Christina Collins appeared on several occasions to be afraid of some violence from the crew and at one place she was observed to be sharpening a knife. (This may well have been a red herring, as the knife had subsequently been found safely shut away in her baggage.) He would also endeavour to prove not only violence but also coarse and threatening language on the part of the accused men. The boat should have arrived at Fazeley at four o'clock on the Monday morning but was two hours late and the unfortunate woman was by that time missing. Her body was found in the canal at Brindley Bank but whether she was thrown into the water or whether she threw herself in were not questions for the jury's present consideration, but whether the accused were guilty of the particular charge of rape.

Evidence would be put forward to show that when the body was discovered, her clothes were considerably rent and torn and her drawers in particular were torn in such a way as to show that she had been used with great violence. Sergeant Ludlow went on to assure the court that he would endeavour to obtain the truth from one of the prisoners (Owen) by admitting him as a Crown witness and stressed that in this, he had no other object but to satisfy public justice. Somewhat surprisingly, Owen then told the court that he would not give evidence, at which Sergeant Ludlow observed that he was not surprised to hear him say so!

The canal bend at Brindley Bank. (Author's collection)

Robert Collins was the first witness. He appeared to be in a great deal of distress, weeping copiously and giving the impression to the people crowded into the public gallery of being hardly able to bear the sight of the accused in the dock. He confirmed that the body was indeed that of his late wife, and that although it was dreadfully disfigured, he recognised her from a mark on the ear.

Elizabeth Grice, the dead women's former employer, was next to enter the witness box and said that although Christina did not possess very good clothes, they were always neat and in a good state of repair. In addition, she was a very delicate kind of person. Cross-examined by Mr Godson, she denied ever having heard Christina claim any connection with the stage or the Covent Garden Theatre. (Whether this connection with the stage was true or not, it hardly seemed relevant to the people crowded into the courtroom.)

William Brookes, a porter in the employ of Pickford's at Stoke-on-Trent, claimed to hear George Thomas use extremely obscene language to the woman, making it quite clear that he had designs on Christina. He also heard her say 'Leave me alone. I'll not have anything to do with you.'

Hugh Cordwell also said that Christina had complained to him that the men were drunk and might 'meddle with her.' Other witnesses, including John Tansley, went into the witness box to give evidence of the rough treatment that the deceased woman had experienced aboard the *Staffordshire Knot*.

Ann Mills, wife of the lockkeeper at Hoo Mill lock, told the court that she had been awakened by a peculiar cry, which she first thought was that of a child but on looking out of the window, saw a boat in the lock with a woman sitting on the cabin. One of the boatmen called out that she had 'been in the cut.'

Then it was young Muston's turn to give evidence, which he did, looking thoroughly frightened. He said that he had missed the woman after Hoo Mill lock between three and four o'clock in the morning, and in reply to his query concerning her whereabouts, Owen had told him that 'he was afeart she was drowned.' Cross-examined by Mr Beadon, Muston said that Ellis was asleep when the boat reached Brindley Bank and when he awoke at Fradley Junction, he would not believe that Christina was dead and searched the boat for her, without success.

John Bladon, an employee of the Trent & Mersey Navigation at Rugeley, told the court that there was a defined course of action for a captain to take if he lost a passenger, including making an entry on the way-bill, which every boat carried. When the *Staffordshire Knot* passed him on the morning of 17 June, no mention had been made to him of any loss.

George Thomas and William Ellis then gave their accounts of what had happened on the *Staffordshire Knot*. Both claimed they had not seen the woman leave the boat or to have seen Owen pulling her from the water as he said he had done. Ellis also said that he had heard Owen swearing at Christina.

James Owen, who repeated the story he had told at the inquest, followed them. He claimed to have been 'muddled' through drink for most of the time but could recall that Thomas had been trying to molest the woman when the boat reached Haywood lock, and shortly afterwards the woman had attempted to jump into the canal. He had caught hold of her and hauled her back into the boat and remained talking to her until Colwich lock, after which he took up the steering and the woman went missing.

At this stage, George Thomas was recalled and claimed that it was James Owen who had been responsible for the bad language directed at the deceased woman. At Fradley, Owen had told Charles Robotham that there was a passenger missing and on the way to Fazeley, Owen had tried to get the other two men to swear that the woman had left the boat at Colwich lock.

Owen, re-examined, denied this and claimed that he had caught Thomas and Ellis going through the woman's boxes and that it was them who had suggested that they should say she got out at Colwich. By now it was clear to the court that the accused were each desperately trying to place the blame on each other.

That concluded the case for the prosecution, which Mr Godson, for Owen, immediately announced was no case at all. The judge seemed to agree for he announced that so far as he was concerned, there was no more evidence of rape than of murder and he thought that there was not a case to go before the jury. He proceeded to tell the jury:

Gentlemen, I in common with you, may suppose that foul play took place on board that boat and about it that night. We may imagine that dreadful deeds were done with regard to this unhappy woman, but in this realm of England, we do not go on mere suspicion; we do not convict except the charge is supported by proofs. The charges are that all three ravished this unhappy woman, but where is the evidence of this woman being ravished at all? You have not heard one word about the state of her person. There is no proof of violence having been committed upon her. It is true that Owen is said to have implied that Thomas raped and murdered her, but whatever suspicion that language may raise in your minds and mine, it is no evidence in law against Thomas, nor is the statement of any one of the prisoner's evidence against another, though it is evidence against himself. I am bound to tell you that there is no proof of their having committed the crime of which they stand charged in this indictment.

With that, the jury returned a verdict of 'Not Guilty.'

At this stage, Mr Sergeant Ludlow applied for a postponement of the charge of murder until the next Assizes, on the ground that if it were not, then a most material piece of evidence would be wanting. One Joseph Orgill, who had at some time been handcuffed to James Owen in prison, was currently locked up in the county gaol on a charge of bigamy and could not be produced in court, but before the next Assizes an application would be made to the Secretary of State for a free pardon, which would then allow him to be a competent witness. All three counsels for the defence resisted this application but the case was postponed to appear before Mr Baron Gurney on 16 March. This time the three men were charged with 'The wilful murder of Christina Collins by casting, pushing and throwing the said Collins into the canal by which means the said Christina Collins was choked, suffocated and drowned.' The accused all pleaded 'Not Guilty' and retained the same counsel. The initial evidence was more or less the same as in the first hearing, and then the recently pardoned Joseph Orgill went into the witness box. He told the court that while he was in gaol, before his own trial, he had occupied a cell with James Owen, who had blurted out his story and had accused Thomas and Ellis of attacking the woman and 'mauling her to death.'

After evidence of the post-mortem, which confirmed death by drowning, counsel gave their summing up on both sides, followed by the judge, who warned the jury that in the whole of his experience he had never met with a case which made a larger demand upon the patience, the attention and the discrimination of a jury. Before they could find a verdict of guilty, they must be fully satisfied that the accused threw her into the water and that they effected her death in that way and no other. The evidence of the boy Muston must be received with great caution. He had been confined in the gaol with two of the prisoners and the jury would also recall that he had claimed not to hear any cries from the woman at Hoo Mill lock, although they had been loud enough to disturb the sleep of the lockkeeper's wife.

Without the evidence of Orgill, the evidence amounted to this: that the woman was taken on board a boat navigated by the three accused men and that her dead body was found in the canal at 5 a.m., still warm. Undoubtedly, as a passenger she was under the care of the persons navigating that boat and they had a duty towards her. Evidence had been given that Thomas had vowed that as his captain had had connexion with the woman, he would do the same and there was heard an entreaty from the woman 'not to attempt her.' There was a question from a witness as to whether she had a protector on the boat, and one of the boatmen answered that she had – her husband – an obvious lie.

The jury must take the whole of the evidence into consideration and if that convinced them that the prisoners were guilty of the murder of this woman by drowning and not by any other means, then they would find them guilty, but if they entertained a fair and reasonable doubt that they did not actually drown her, however disgusted they might feel at their conduct in other respects, and however might be the suspicions that rested upon them, they would find the accused not guilty.

The jury then retired but were back within three quarters of an hour with a unanimous verdict of guilty, whereupon the judge donned the black cap and pronounced sentence of death.

In the event, William Ellis was not hanged, his sentence being transmuted to transportation to Australia for life, this good news being given to him just as he and his two colleagues were receiving the last rites on the morning of the execution. The other two were led out in front of a crowd estimated at some thousands and it was reported that as they hung, their bodies were 'much convulsed'. The executioner was the famous William Calcraft, assisted by a prisoner from Stafford Gaol, George Smith, who volunteered for the job because Calcraft's regular assistant was too drunk to take part! Smith was later to act as executioner to William Palmer (*see* Chapter Two). Afterwards, William Ellis was seen viewing the dead bodies of his companions and was said to have been much affected by the spectacle.

The present-day site of the 'Bloody Steps.' (Author's collection)

In a letter to the *Staffordshire Advertiser*, the vicar of Haughton, the Revd Charles Smith Royds, lamented that the boatmen had to work on Sundays and were therefore prevented from attending church service. It would seem that the coroner's jury were of a similar mind, for they wrote a strong letter to the coroner expressing 'their decided conviction of the great impropriety of the carrying on of business by land and water upon the Sunday in the same manner as the other days.'

William Ellis got off lightly, although transportation to Australia was certainly no picnic, but Owen and Thomas were convicted on the flimsiest of evidence. It is clear that the ruffianly crew were drunk on that fateful journey, but that was probably their usual state. Although no evidence was produced, it seems likely that other unaccompanied women passengers had had to suffer the drunken attentions of the crew members from time to time and Christina's situation might not have been anything out of the ordinary. The medical evidence was sketchy and we have no idea of the professional competence of Dr Barnett, or precisely what he found in his examination of Christina's body. He mentioned no marks of a struggle, which would surely have been evident if Christina had been fighting for her virtue, but on the other hand, if she

Christina Collins' gravestone in Rugeley churchyard. (Author's collection)

threw herself into the canal, why did she not just wade to the nearest bank and climb out?

Ever since the murder, there has been a belief that when the body of Christina Collins was being carried up the steps at Brindley Bank, her blood stained the steps indelibly. The original steps have long since been replaced by concrete, but are still known among the locals as the 'Bloody Steps' and it is said that on 17 June 1939, exactly one hundred years after the crime, a Rugeley woman and her daughter saw a figure in breeches and with hair tied back, walk on the water and disappear through the steps.

Today, the grave of Christina Collins at St Augustine's Church, Rugeley, bears a large headstone with the inscription:

To the memory of Christina Collins, wife of Robert Collins, London. Who having been most barbarously treated was found dead in the canal in this Parish on 17 June 1839. Aged thirty-seven years. This stone is erected by some individuals of the Parish of Rugeley in commemoration of the end of this unhappy woman.

As a modern postscript, the story of Christina Collins was the basis for Colin Dexter's Inspector Morse book, *The Wench Is Dead*, with the action translated from Rugeley to Oxford. This author does not agree with Mr Dexter's conclusions!

2

THE RUGELEY
POISONER

Rugeley, 1855

William Palmer was born into a well-to-do family in Rugeley on 21 October 1824, the sixth of seven children, his parents being Sarah and Joseph Palmer. Joseph was a sawyer by trade and had the reputation of being a hard man and more than a bit of a rogue. They occupied a large house, rather curiously known as 'The Yard', situated just across the road from the parish church, St Augustine's, and in due course William followed his siblings to the Rugeley Free Grammar School, situated nearby. His reputation there was poor and he was considered by his schoolmates to be a thoroughly bad boy, who cheated whenever it suited him. He was never short of money and had far more than his fellow pupils could command and it was said that he did not baulk at robbing members of his own family if they were so foolish as to leave cash lying loose.

William's father died when he was 12 years old, leaving his widow well provided for. According to some accounts, she was worth over £70,000 at the time and William promptly made up his mind to devote his life's work to relieving his long-suffering mother of as much of her fortune as he could manage. At the age of 17, he went to work in Liverpool, as an apprentice to Evans & Co., chemists of Lord Street. This job lasted less than three months, Palmer being dismissed for theft. From there, he went on to study medicine and qualified by the skin of his teeth in August 1846. That year, after returning from London where he finished his studies, Palmer met a man named George Abley, a plumber and glazier, whose tombstone stands today in the churchyard of St Michaels and all Angels, Colwich. Palmer is supposed to have invited Abley to the Lamb and Flag public house at Little Haywood, where he plied the man with drink, making sure that Abley drank nothing but 'doubles'. In quick time, Abley was drunk and refused to drink any more, whereupon Palmer offered him half a sovereign if he could down one more glass of neat brandy. Taking the bet in his fuddled state, Abley downed the glass and promptly staggered outside, to much laughter from Palmer and his friends. About an hour later, the unfortunate Abley was found in a collapsed

A contemporary engraving of Mrs Palmer's house. (Author's collection)

Mrs Palmer's house, 2007. (Author's collection)

condition and was carried home, where he died later that evening. There was some suspicion locally that Palmer had more than a passing interest in Abley's good-looking wife at the time, but nothing was ever proven.

A year later, Palmer married Annie Thornton, a spinster and the illegitimate daughter of Mary Thornton (also known as Ann), who in turn was the mistress of a Colonel Brookes. When the colonel died in 1834, after committing suicide by shooting himself, young Annie came into £8,000 and no doubt William Palmer thought her something of a catch. Upon their marriage, they decided to settle in Rugeley and took a house in Market Street, opposite the Talbot Arms, which they rented at £25 per annum. The double-fronted house offered spacious accommodation and was slightly set back from the street, with railings in front and a small garden. There, Palmer set himself up in business as a medical practitioner and before long he was able to take on a full-time assistant, Benjamin Thirlby.

Palmer wasted no time in borrowing money from his mother-in-law, a good looking but vile-tempered and hard drinking woman known for decency's sake as Mrs Thornton. In January 1849 she came to Rugeley on a visit, but within two weeks she was dead from the effects of drink, aged 50; the death certificate signed by Dr Bamford giving the cause as 'apoplexy.' The local gossips whispered that Palmer had expected his wife to inherit a tidy bit of property when her mother died, but in this he was disappointed, although Annie did continue to receive an annual income from the estate.

Dr William Palmer.
(Author's collection)

Perhaps buoyed up by his mother's wealth, some of which he expected to inherit in due course, Palmer took up horseracing which naturally led him to gambling. One day, at the races, he came across Leonard Bladen, who worked for Charrington's Brewery. Bladen was inveigled into lending the doctor money, something that he soon regretted, as it proved difficult to get back. The two men visited Chester races in 1850, where Bladen won a lot of money and afterwards sent word to his wife that he was going to Rugeley to get what Palmer owed him and that he expected to come home with around £1,000. While at Palmer's house, Bladen was taken ill and was soon in agony, dying on 10 May. To the surprise of his wife, he had little money on his person when he was examined after death and his betting books were missing. This was highly convenient for Palmer as there was now no evidence to show exactly what his financial relationship with Bladen had been, and Bladen's wife was astonished to be told by Palmer that her late husband had owed him £60, especially as in his letter to her, Bladen had claimed that the doctor owed him £600! The cause of death was given as 'Injury of the hip joint, 5 or 6 months; abscess in the pelvis,' (he had previously been involved in an accident when he was hit by a runaway cart). Palmer was noted on the certificate as being 'present at the death.'

Meantime, William and Annie were adding to their family, and eventually had five children, although four of them did not reach their first birthday: Elizabeth, expiring on 6 January 1851 from 'convulsions,' aged 10 weeks; Henry, expiring on 6 January 1852 from 'convulsions,' aged 1 month; Frank, expiring on 19 December 1852 from 'convulsions,' aged 7 hours; and John, who died on 27 January 1854 after living for only 3 days, again from the ubiquitous 'convulsions.' These deaths would not have excited much comment at the time, as infant mortality was high and many families, after a dozen years of marriage, would have had more children under the ground than above it, although after the trial, there were those who suggested that Palmer may have made away with the infants, viewing them as an unnecessary household expense.

By 1854, due to his betting activities, Palmer was deeper in debt than ever, and his creditors were beginning to make life uncomfortable for him. In addition, he had been forging bills in his mother's name and these now totalled several thousand pounds. Should this be discovered, the spectre of ruin and the debtor's prison loomed.

Palmer decided that he would have to take firm action and conceived a plan to kill his wife, after first insuring her life for a considerable sum. At that time, the rules about insurable interest were by no means as strict as they are now (an alteration that was eventually brought about by this case) and he applied to take out several policies with various companies. Not all the companies approached were keen to do business with the good doctor, but the Prince of Wales Insurance Company eventually issued a policy in the sum of £13,000 on the life of Annie Palmer, in favour of her husband, the first premium for which was £750.

A contemporary photograph of Dr William Palmer's house, Rugeley. (Author's collection)

Dr William Palmer's house, 2007. (Author's collection)

Mrs Palmer duly obliged by passing away on 29 September 1854, aged 27, ostensibly from cholera, which was endemic in this country at that time and so caused little comment. She was buried, watched by a large crowd, in the Palmer family vault at the east end of the parish church and soon her grieving husband was steeling himself to apply for the proceeds of her life policy, which were promptly turned over to him by the insurance company. Most of this money quickly passed into the pockets of Palmer's creditors and by early 1855, Palmer was again raising money by virtue of forged bills on his mother's account, but finding it increasingly difficult to do so. The men who discounted these bills for Palmer, named Pratt and Padwick, were now beginning to press for their money and threatening to seek an audience with Palmer's mother, something that he needed desperately to avoid, so he now turned his attention to his brother, Walter, a corn-merchant and a drunkard, who had twice been made bankrupt. Walter was separated from his wife, due to his intemperate habits, and was living in a small house in Stafford. Using Pratt as a reference, Palmer attempted to take out policies on Walter's life for the truly incredible sum of £84,000 and, hardly surprisingly, found this impossible. However, fortunately for the doctor, the somewhat gullible Prince of Wales Insurance Company issued a policy in the sum of £14,000 and it was Pratt who paid the first (and only) premium of £780, taking a commission of £120 for himself and surely involving himself in a venture that he must have known was illegal. Presumably by now he had also realised that there was little likelihood of him getting his money back from Palmer without so doing. Walter Palmer was now drinking several bottles of gin and brandy a day, and waking up during the night to consume even more, all purchased for him by his brother. On Thursday 16 August 1855, Palmer was able to write in his diary 'Walter died' and Walter joined his ancestors in the family vault on the following Monday.

Palmer now attempted to cash in the Prince of Wales policy but this time found the company reluctant to part with its money, still evidently smarting from the £13,000 they had paid out in respect of Palmer's wife. In due course, two inspectors, Messrs Simpson and Field, were dispatched to Rugeley to make enquiries and were also asked to look into the matter of an application for an insurance policy on the life of one George Bate, or Bates, variously described as an under-groom and a farmer. He was said to have been in Palmer's employment between September and November 1855, being responsible for looking after the doctor's horses, although his terms of service appeared to have been rather vague and he was evidently reliant on Palmer dropping him the odd sovereign from time to time. In September 1855, he had a discussion with the doctor about insuring his life for £10,000 and an application form was produced which he signed and had witnessed by two of Palmer's racing cronies, Samuel Cheshire, the postmaster at Rugeley, and John Parsons Cook.

The Palmer family plot, c. 1925. (Author's collection)

All that remains of the Palmer family plot in 2007. (Author's collection)

Simpson and Field found discrepancies in the details on Bate's policy, which had him described as a farmer with private means amounting to £400 per annum, although to the inspectors he appeared to be just a farm labourer, hoeing turnips. In addition, Bate insisted that the insurance on his life was only for £4,000, of which he was to have £1,000 within the year, which heightened their suspicions even more.

They now advised the Prince of Wales Insurance Company not to pay out on Walter Palmer's policy and visited the doctor to tell him so to his face, boldly saying that they had great suspicion that Walter had been poisoned and that they would recommend that there should be an enquiry, at which Palmer would figure. Whether this was a ploy by the insurance company to frighten Palmer into giving up any claim to the policy is not clear, but Palmer obviously found this most inconvenient, as his creditors were once more pressing. He was uncomfortably aware that even if he received the whole of the proceeds of the insurance policy, it would be insufficient to keep everybody quiet.

It was then that the doctor decided that he would attempt to sort out all his problems by murdering his race-going friend John Parsons Cook, a sallow young man of indifferent health who, after inheriting some £12,000, had decided to devote his time to spending it. The two men had known each other for a couple of years and regularly visited the racecourses, both men owning racehorses. On Tuesday 13 November 1855, Cook and Palmer attended Shrewsbury races, where Cook's horse, Polestar, came first in the major handicap of the day, winning Cook some £3,000. That evening, Cook threw a party at the Raven Hotel, where he and Palmer were staying, although Palmer himself did not stay long to share his friend's good fortune and returned to Rugeley.

The following day, Palmer received a letter from the moneylender, Pratt, demanding that a significant sum of money should be handed over to him at once, failing which Pratt would go straight to Palmer's mother and ask awkward questions. The doctor at once returned to Shrewsbury and on the evening of Wednesday 14 November he was sitting with Cook and a few friends, including wine merchant Mr Ishmael Fisher, and law stationer Thomas Jones. When a tray of brandies was brought in, Cook, who liked his drink, swallowed his but immediately complained that it burnt his throat. Palmer picked up the nearly empty glass and sipped at it, handing the glass to one of his companions, George Read, saying, 'Taste it. There's nothing in it. Cook says it is drugged.' Read replied that he could see nothing in the glass, as Palmer appeared to have drained it!

Cook continued to complain of feeling ill and went off to his room, accompanied by two of the company, George Herring and Ishmael Fisher, where he vomited copiously. 'I believe that damned Palmer has been dosing me,' he told his friends. Later a doctor was sent for but his ministrations had

WILLIAM PALMER OF RUGELEY.

A contemporary cartoon of Dr Palmer at the races. (Author's collection)

little effect and Cook was still ill the following morning. On Thursday, Palmer had a horse named Nettle running and had backed it heavily. The horse failed, making Palmer's condition even more desperate, and he and Cook travelled back to Rugeley, where Cook immediately took to his bed at the Talbot Arms, just across the road from Palmer's house. On Friday, he was well enough to have lunch with Palmer and his solicitor, Jeremiah Smith (usually referred to as Jere), and on Saturday morning Palmer ordered some coffee at the hotel and offered some to Cook, who took it. After this, the vomiting started all over again and he became very ill, Palmer being ever-present and careful of his friend's health, all the while solicitously administering food and medicine.

On Sunday morning, Palmer called in the 80-year-old Dr Bamford, who made up sedative pills for Cook, and later in the day Jere Smith sent over some soup to Palmer's house, which he suggested Cook might like. Palmer took this to his friend and once again the vomiting started, so the remainder was sent down to the hotel kitchen to be kept warm. The chambermaid, Elizabeth Mills, thought that the soup gave off an appetising smell and drank a couple of spoonfuls, whereupon she, too, was taken ill with vomiting. Later in the day, the remainder of the soup was taken back up to Cook's room, where he suffered further bouts of sickness after drinking more of it.

The following day, Palmer went up to London to meet his racing friend George Herring (a well-to-do commission agent who died a millionaire in 1906), and arranged with Herring to collect on Cook's behalf a series of bets totalling nearly £2,000. Palmer promptly paid £800 of this money to his own creditors, Pratt and Padwick, and was now left in possession of some £1,200 of Cook's money. Returning to Rugeley, he bought three grains of strychnine from the surgery of a Dr Salt, which he took to his own surgery, and, making the poison up into two pills, he then went over to the Talbot Arms and gave them to Cook. In a later letter from Palmer to Jere Smith, the doctor insisted that the pills had come from Dr Bamford.

On Tuesday 20 November 1855, Cook was again very ill and at Palmer's request, Dr Jones was called at 2 p.m. and stayed in the room, intending to pass the night there with his patient. At around midnight, Jones undressed and settled down to a fitful sleep, but had hardly closed his eyes before Cook called urgently for Dr Palmer, who arrived shortly afterwards and administered two ammonia pills. A terrible scene now ensued, with Cook going into convulsions, his body bent upwards like a bow as he screamed that he was suffocating. Gradually, the convulsions lessened and at 1 a.m. the mortal sufferings of John Parsons Cook ended.

The following day, Dr Jones went to London to contact Cook's stepfather, Mr William Stevens, a retired merchant, and returned to Rugeley with him. Together, they went to the Talbot Arms where they met Palmer and proceeded to view the body. Afterwards, Stevens was alarmed to hear from Palmer that there were outstanding bills of some £4,000 that Cook had been responsible for. An attempt was made to find Cook's betting book, which now seemed to have disappeared, but Palmer dismissed this as immaterial, claiming that all bets were off when someone died.

Stevens then wrote to the Stafford coroner, asking for an inquest to be held into Cook's death as soon as possible. He also wrote to Dr Harland, a physician from Stafford, asking him to conduct the post-mortem. He was particularly keen to ensure that any specimens taken at the post-mortem were to be forwarded to Dr Alfred Swaine Taylor at Guy's Hospital, one of the foremost poisons experts in the land. Despite this, Palmer was able to obtain a death certificate from the aged Dr Bamford, which stated that Cook had died from apoplexy.

An engraving of the Talbot Arms, c. 1856. (Author's collection)

The Talbot Arms (now renamed The Shrew), 2007. (Author's collection)

The post-mortem on Cook was held at the Talbot Arms on 26 November 1855, watched by a crowd of onlookers, including Jere Smith and the local postmaster, Samuel Cheshire. Overseen by Dr Harland, the autopsy was conducted by Mr Charles Devonshire, a medical student, and Mr Charles Newton, an unqualified assistant to Mr Salt, the Rugeley chemist. Why such inexperienced practitioners should have been allowed to conduct this vital examination is not clear and there was some suspicion that Newton had partaken of more than a few brandies before the examination started. While Devonshire was in the act of removing the stomach, Palmer was seen to bump against Newton who in turn collided with Devonshire, who spilled some of the stomach contents back into the body. The remainder he placed in a jar, sealing it with a pig's bladder; other organs of the body were similarly dealt with. Suddenly, Devonshire noticed that the jar containing the stomach contents was missing and Palmer admitted that he had moved it out of the way, for 'safe keeping'. When the jar was brought back into the room, Devonshire noticed that there was a cut in the sealing bladder, although none of the contents appeared to have been lost.

The jars were then sent off to Dr Taylor, who complained that the contents were in such a state that he could not deal with them and requested further samples. These were taken at a second post-mortem on 29 November and sent off to London.

Samuel Cheshire, the postmaster, having agreed with Palmer that he would intercept any letters written to the coroner, produced one from Professor Taylor, stating that he had found no traces of strychnine, prussic acid or opium in the samples sent to him. Palmer thereupon rewarded the postmaster with a gift of fish and game and then took the astonishing step of writing to the coroner, asking him to bring in a verdict of death by natural causes and enclosing a £10 note! Cheshire was ultimately prosecuted for interfering with the mail and received a sentence of two years.

The adjourned inquest was renewed on Friday 14 December, with coroner William Webb Ward, when Dr Taylor confirmed that he had found no trace of strychnine, although he suspected that Palmer had administered strychnine in the pills that he gave to Cook on the Monday evening. Presumably, the coroner and the jury accepted this curiously ambivalent statement in view of Dr Taylor's eminence; certainly no one seems to have queried it. On 15 December, the jury retired for a very short time and returned with a verdict that the 'Deceased died of poison wilfully administered to him by William Palmer', a verdict which, at that time, could still legally be handed down at an inquest. The coroner was later to be censured for the way in which he had allowed the inquest to be conducted.

Palmer was at the time in bed, possibly feigning illness to avoid his creditors, who were now pressing even more. A warrant had been taken out against him by money-lender Padwick, on a charge of forgery, and Palmer

The death certificate of John Parsons Cook, certifying death from 'apoplexy'. (Crown Copyright)

was effectively now under house arrest, guarded by two police constables until he was well enough to be taken to Stafford Gaol.

During his stay there, he affected to go on hunger strike, but was soon persuaded against this by the governor of the gaol, who warned Palmer that unless he changed his attitude, he would cause him to be force-fed. Palmer remained at Stafford until just before his trial was to commence, when he was taken to Newgate Prison in London.

A special Act of Parliament had been hurriedly enacted to enable the trial to be moved from Stafford to London on account of the tremendous furore that had been created in the newspapers of the time, which freely rehearsed the evidence and accused Dr Palmer of numerous crimes, including the deaths of his children. It was felt that he would not be able to receive a fair trial in Stafford because of this. Meanwhile, the Home Secretary had ordered further examinations of the bodies of Palmer's wife and brother, Walter, and that inquest took place on 22 December 1855. The bodies were exhumed and carried across the road to the Talbot Inn (not the Talbot Arms) where the coffins were opened in the presence of Dr Monckton, Dr Bamford, the coroner and twenty-three local jurymen. Mrs Palmer's corpse was very well preserved but that of Walter Palmer was considerably decomposed and the smell that arose when the coffin was opened was said to have existed for years afterwards and to have been responsible for the eventual closure of the inn!

The condition of Walter Palmer's body made it impossible for a further examination to take place and the jury eventually decided that they could return no other verdict than the original one of apoplexy. On Mrs Palmer, however, the jury had no such qualms and probably largely on the evidence of Professor Taylor, who stated that he had found antimony in all the organs of the body, they brought in a verdict of wilful murder against William Palmer, for poisoning his wife.

Palmer's trial on a charge of murdering John Parsons Cook started on 14 May 1856, to great excitement. The three trial judges appointed for what was plainly seen as a major criminal case were the elderly Lord Chief Justice Campbell, together with Baron Alderson and Mr Justice Cresswell. Leading for Palmer's defence was the imposing quartet of Mr Serjeant Shee, the MP for Kilkenny, assisted by Mr Grove QC with Mr Gray and Mr Kenealey. For the Crown appeared the Attorney General, Sir Alexander Cockburn, as was usual in poisoning cases, with Mr Edward James QC assisted by Mr Bodkin, Mr Welsby and Mr Huddleston, another formidable team.

Evidence was first received from those people who had been present at Shrewsbury when Cook complained of the brandy burning his throat. Ishmael Fisher told the court that Cook had given him between £700 and £800 to look after while he was ill, money that later disappeared. Others present all testified to the throat burning episode and Ann Brookes, stated to be 'a lady who attended races' (and who admitted that she went there without the consent of her husband!) said that she was on her way to Palmer's room when she saw the doctor standing in the passageway holding a glass tumbler which had a small amount of a colourless liquid in it, although he did not seem to be concerned that she had seen him with it. Elizabeth Mills, the chambermaid at the Talbot Arms, told the court how she had drunk a small amount of the soup, sent in by Palmer, and had been ill afterwards, with much vomiting. She also said that after moving from Rugeley to London, five weeks after the death of Cook, she had been visited six or seven times by Cook's stepfather, Mr Stevens, who was sometimes accompanied by his solicitor, Mr Gardner, and Captain John Hayes Hatton, Chief Constable for Stafford.

Serjeant Shee questioned Elizabeth very closely on the subject of Mr Stevens' visits, saying pointedly that 'Mr Stevens is not a man in your station' and being plainly puzzled how this 'gentleman' could have called to see her just to find out how she was getting on in London. The girl defended herself stoutly, denying that Mr Stevens had ever mentioned anything to her about Cook's death and rather mysteriously mentioning that there were other subjects of conversation between them, although she declined to say what they were. Curiously, she does not appear to have been pressed for any further information on this subject.

The Talbot Inn, where inquests where held on Dr Palmer's mother and brother, Walter. Sixteen years previously, this had also been the site of the inquest on Christina Collins. (Author's collection)

The original courtroom at the Old Bailey, where Dr Palmer was tried. (Author's collection)

Both the report on the trial published in *The Times* and the *Notable British Trials* book on the case give graphic accounts of Cook's last struggles, as related by the girl. At about quarter to midnight, she was startled to hear the noise of violent screaming coming from Cook's room and on entering she found Cook sitting up in bed. He claimed that he was unable to lie down and asked her to fetch Dr Palmer. She went on, 'His body, his hands and neck were moving, a sort of jumping or jerking. His head was back. Sometimes he would throw back his head upon the pillow, and then he would raise himself again. This jumping and jerking was all over his body and he appeared to have great difficulty in breathing. The balls of his eyes were much projected and it was difficult for him to speak. He screamed three or four times while I was in the room and he called aloud "Murder" twice. He asked me to rub one hand and I found it stiff.' Palmer then appeared and brought with him some pills that he administered to Cook in a little wine. Cook appeared to have some difficulty in swallowing them and on Palmer's instructions Elizabeth attempted to give him a teaspoonful of toast and water. This she had some difficulty with, as Cook's body was convulsing and at one time the spoon was fast between his teeth. Palmer then gave him a glass containing a dark, heavy-looking liquid, which Cook drank but almost immediately vomited back again.

Dr William Henry Jones gave evidence that Cook's health had not been very robust. He confirmed that on the night Cook called out for Dr Palmer, his friend started having convulsions which lasted five or ten minutes and his whole body was bent upwards like a bow. He gradually weakened and his heart ceased at about 1 o'clock in the morning. It was his view that Cook had died of tetanus.

The court burst into excited conversation when it was announced that the next witness to be called would be Charles Newton, the assistant to Mr Salt, the chemist, and the man who had sold strychnine to Dr Palmer on 19 November. He stated that he had also seen Palmer purchase more strychnine in a neighbouring shop on the following day. When asked why he had not entered Palmer's purchase in the poisons book, as he was required to do, he said that his employer had 'fallen out' with Dr Palmer because his assistant, Ben Thirlby, had left to work for Palmer and he thought that Mr Salt would be angry with him for supplying it. He also claimed that Palmer had quizzed him about the action of strychnine and the amount needed to kill a dog. Lord Campbell, in his summing up, was to emphasise that Newton had made no mention of strychnine at the coroner's court and in fact had only mentioned it in the previous twenty-four hours when he was on his way to London to give evidence. However, the judge then went on to stress that Newton had no possible motive for lying on this important point.

Charles Joseph Roberts, apprentice to Mr Hawkins, druggist of Rugeley, then gave evidence of a sale of strychnine to Palmer and confessed that he also had not troubled to enter the purchase in the poisons book, as he was supposed to do. The cavalier attitude of Rugeley chemist's assistants to the requirements of the law seems remarkable, although the fact that Palmer was a doctor and well known to both men was perhaps partly responsible.

Thomas Pratt, solicitor and money lender, disclosed that he had been lending money to Palmer at 60 per cent interest and Rugeley bank manager, Mr Stawbridge, told the court that Palmer's bank balance was less than £9 on 3 November 1855 and that nothing had been credited to the account since that date.

On the fourth day of the trial, the medical evidence was called and there was some considerable discussion as to the varying types of tetanus, which both prosecution and defence agreed had been the cause of death of John Parsons Cook. (This referred to the so-called 'tetanus due to strychnine' where the symptoms of strychnine poisoning bear a strong resemblance to tetanus but are more acute and less prolonged than in a case of tetanus.) Dr Bamford was too unwell to give evidence in person, as he was suffering from cholera and his evidence was read out in court. It was his opinion that death had been due to congestion of the brain, a theory that was roughly cast aside by subsequent medical witnesses. Throughout the day, a succession of medical men came and went, the general opinion being that Cook had died from tetanus due to strychnine, and they were followed by witnesses who had seen others die of that poison and who could describe the symptoms.

On the fifth day, there was great interest as the Attorney General examined the eminent Dr Alfred Taylor. He announced with great solemnity that he had made strychnine the subject of his attentions, although he was forced to admit that he had never seen the condition in a human being – all his experience had been based on animal experiments. Despite this, he announced to the jury that he had written a book on the subject.

He confirmed that he and his assistant, Dr Rees, had searched for a number of poisons in those of Cook's remains that had been sent to him, including prussic and oxalic acids, morphia, strychnine, hemlock, arsenic, antimony and other mineral poisons generally. He only found traces of antimony, but qualified this by telling the court that the remains sent to him were in a most unfavourable condition for finding strychnine, if it had been there. The stomach had been completely cut from end to end, all the contents were gone and the whole of what remained must have been shaken up very much on the journey to London. If there had been any strychnine, he would have expected it to be found in the contents of the stomach. Antimony (Tartar emetic) had been found, although not enough to cause death. When cross-examined, he had to admit, rather lamely, that he did not know any other cause of the symptoms exhibited at the last by Cook, other than strychnine.

Other doctors followed, including Professor Robert Christison of the University of Edinburgh, who also agreed that he had never seen a fatal case of strychnine poisoning in a human being. Again, the greater part of his experience had been on animals, but he said that Cook's symptoms appeared to him to be very like those he had heard of in other cases. (Such vague statements as this would be stamped on hard by a modern-day judge.)

Further medical evidence was taken on the sixth day as to the symptoms of lockjaw and the remainder of the day was taken up with evidence concerning Palmer's financial transactions with the moneylenders, the forging of his mother's name and the fact that there was nothing in his papers to show joint transactions between him and Cook.

On day seven, Mr Serjeant Shee stood up to begin the defence, with a speech that lasted several hours. An imposing figure, with a shock of iron-grey hair and long sideburns, he immediately told the court that only once before had he taken part in a trial for a man's life and that he felt very much the burden that was now laid on him. (Palmer's trial seems to have been dominated by people who admitted they knew little of what they were talking about!) Shee emphasised that the Crown's case, that in the second week of November the prisoner, having decided to get rid of John Parsons Cook, deliberately prepared his body for deadly poison by the slower poison of antimony and afterwards despatched him with the deadly poison of strychnine, was supported entirely by circumstantial evidence.

'But,' he told the jury, 'strychnine was not found in Cook's body. If he died from strychnine poisoning, he died within two hours of the administration to him of a very strong dose of it and there was no reason to suppose that there was any dilution of it in the stomach or any ejection of it by vomiting. Never, therefore, were circumstances more favourable for detection of the poison, and yet none was found.' (This, of course, was a telling point and should have weighed heavily in Palmer's favour with the jury, although they appear to have taken little notice of it, in the event.)

In an impassioned plea to the jury, he told them, 'I do not entertain the smallest doubt that you must be convinced of the innocence of this man and I will never believe that it was in the interest of William Palmer or that he thought it was in his interest, to destroy Cook.' He finished by reading out a letter that Palmer had written to his wife, Annie, while he was away studying to become a doctor:

> My Dearest Annie,
> I snatch a moment to write to your dear, dear little self. I need scarcely say the principal inducement I have to work is the desire of getting my studies finished, so as to be able to press your dear little form in my arms.
> >   With best, best love, dearest Annie, your own William.

The accused was, Shee told the jury, 'a young man who loved a young woman for her own sake... Such an affection as that would in almost all natures be a sure antidote against guilt and such, gentlemen, is the man whom it is my duty to defend.' An imposing way to end his speech although, once more, the jury gave little heed to it.

Then, no fewer than fifteen medical men gave their evidence on behalf of the defence, few of whom had ever seen a case of strychnine poisoning in a human being, but several supported the defence's suggestion that if there had been any strychnine, it would have been found in the stomach contents, (which, of course, had 'gone missing').

Sadler George Myatt deposed that he was with Palmer and Cook at Shrewsbury races and lodged with them at the Raven Hotel. He remembered seeing Cook drink some brandy and that he complained that it burned his throat, but he was quite certain that had anything been put in the brandy by anyone, he would have seen it and that on no occasion had Palmer left the room carrying a glass of brandy.

The final witness for the defence was Jere Smith, who gave a very bad impression. He insisted that he had no recollection of Palmer asking him to attest a proposal on the life of his brother Walter with the Prince of Wales Insurance Company for £13,000, nor another at the Solicitors and General office for a similar figure. When questioned, he also denied any involvement with a policy in the Universal office for £13,000 on Walter Palmer's life, but when shown an assignment of this policy by Walter to Dr Palmer, with his signature on it, he grew vague and muttered that though it did look like his signature, it was a good imitation and he had some doubt that it was not his handwriting.

It was now the tenth day of the trial and the Attorney General stood up to give a long and masterful final speech for the prosecution, using his right to address the jury last. He dealt mainly with the question of strychnine but must also have impressed the jury with his demolishment of Jere Smith's evidence. 'I need not say that any evidence would have been better than the evidence of that miserable man whom we saw exhibited today. Such a spectacle I never saw, in my recollection, in a court of justice. He calls himself a man of the legal profession. I blush to number such a man upon its roll... There cannot be a man here who is not convinced that Smith has been mixed up in many a villainy which, if not perpetrated, had been attempted.' Warming to his task, he moved on to Dr Bamford; 'I speak of that gentleman in terms of perfect respect, but I do him no injustice to say that the vigour of his intellect and his power of observation have been impaired by the advancing hand of time.' This ruthless demolishing of two defence witnesses by the prosecution must have weighed heavily on the minds of all present, and slowly and with equal force the Attorney General took the jury through Palmer's monetary difficulties: the forged bills, the considerable amounts owed to Pratt and Padwick, bills coming in by the day and Pratt, among others, exerting pressure for them to be paid; not forgetting his attempted blackmail of Palmer by threatening to confront his mother, who almost certainly had no inkling of the difficulties in which her son found himself. The jury listened attentively as the picture was built up of a man deeply in debt, struggling to find any means of getting his hands on ready cash. 'Cook,' the Attorney said, 'was Palmer's best friend and Palmer had had the use of all of Cook's money and, at the end, all that Cook had in the world was his winnings at Shrewsbury races.'

The court then adjourned till Monday 26 May when Lord Campbell addressed the jury. He told them that the prosecution alleged that Cook had first of all been 'tampered with' by antimony and then killed by strychnine, whereas the defence alleged that Cook did not die from strychnine poisoning, but from natural causes. The question of motive was not important, as experience showed that crimes were often committed to gain a small pecuniary advantage and to drive off for a time pressing difficulties. The most damning part of the judge's summing up, however, was when he outlined the several purchases of strychnine that Dr Palmer was known to have made, just a short while before John Parsons Cook's health deteriorated.

The summing up extended into the following day and after further advice from his Lordship, the jury retired, taking just one hour and sixteen minutes to arrive at a verdict of 'Guilty.' (A letter from one of the jurymen in *The Times* a few days after the trial explained that nothing was said in the jury room for about fifteen minutes and then each man wrote his own verdict on a piece of paper. When read, all were found to be unanimous.) The other charges on which Palmer was committed, the murders of his wife and his brother, were not proceeded with, in accordance with the usual practice.

Lord Campbell then donned the black cap and pronounced sentence of death, which Palmer received without flinching. He was hastily dressed in prison clothes and taken by train back to Stafford where, upon reaching Stafford station, it was found that there was no vehicle ready to take them to the prison, nor was any prison officer available. Anxious that Palmer should be got behind bars as quickly as practicable, the two accompanying warders decided that they had no alternative but to walk him the few hundred yards to the gaol, even though Palmer was heavily manacled and could walk only with some difficulty, his irons being hidden under a large prison cloak. One of the constables at the scene, PC Thomas Woollaston, was known to Palmer and, at the doctor's request, walked alongside him the whole way.

Palmer was hanged outside Stafford Gaol at 8 a.m. on Saturday 14 June 1856 in front of a massive crowd, an appeal to the Home Secretary having failed. Just before he mounted the scaffold, Palmer was asked by the prison governor if he would not confess his guilt. Palmer replied: 'Cook did not die from strychnine.' The governor, irritated, asked again, 'This is no time for quibbling – did you, or did you not, kill Cook?' The only answer was 'The Lord Chief Justice summed up for poisoning by strychnine.'

The *Staffordshire Advertiser*, in its edition of Saturday 14 June 1856, carried a full account of the execution, and described how Palmer walked

John Parsons Cook's gravestone in Rugeley churchyard. The date of death is one day out. (Author's collection)

Dr Palmer's death mask, made by Mr Bridges, phrenologist of Liverpool. (Author's collection)

firmly to the scaffold, which was hung with black cloth, and positioned himself under the noose. The watching crowd was estimated at 35,000 people, many of whom were the worse for drink, the pubs having been kept open all night. Palmer was dressed in prison clothing, a frieze jacket and trousers with a check shirt, and appeared ghastly pale. The condemned man did not flinch as the executioner, George Smith, placed the rope round his neck and drew the white cap over his face. For a few seconds after the bolt was drawn, the heavy body twitched and then was still. After hanging for the compulsory hour, the corpse was taken down and casts of the head were made by Mr William Bally, phrenologist, and by Mr Bridges of the Phrenological Society of Liverpool. PC Woollaston was again present.

Palmer was the forty-eighth person executed at Stafford and was buried beside the old prison chapel, in a grave lined with quicklime. He is known to be one of 107 men and four women to be buried there. John Parsons Cook was buried in St Augustine's churchyard at Rugeley, and his tombstone can still be seen. The date of death is given as 22 November 1855, which is incorrect as he actually died the day before.

It has been said that the inhabitants of Rugeley were so distressed by the ill fame that had been attached to their town by Palmer that they petitioned the Prime Minister to change its name. Palmerston, for it was he, suggested that they name the town after him, a suggestion that the good Staffordshire citizens declined to take up. As a final postscript, the *Sentinel* for 20 May 1946 carried a small paragraph headed 'Last Link with Palmer the Poisoner.' This related to the presentation by Mrs E. Smith, widow of Dr Edwin Smith, former coroner for South West London and a lecturer in forensic medicine at St Thomas's Hospital, of a prescription, written in Palmer's own hand and signed 'Wm. P.' The prescription was for opium and on the reverse was a chemist's bill for 10d in respect of strychnine and opium.

3

THE WEDDING ANNIVERSARY MURDER

Biddulph Moor, 1900

Forty-year-old coal miner Joseph Arthur Shufflebotham and his 36-year-old wife Elizabeth had both been married before, although neither of their first marriages had been much of a success. The two were married at Biddulph Moor church on 28 December 1899 and between them they had eight children from their first essays into wedlock, aged between 3 and 16 years, and Elizabeth had given birth to their own child about two months previously. Whether it was Joseph's harsh working conditions or the scars that their first marriages had left on them, their second try at marriage was no more successful than their first and Elizabeth soon realised that Joseph was a bit too free with his fists for her liking, and apart from his hot temper, he often accused her of favouring her own children in preference to his.

Elizabeth herself was regarded in the neighbourhood as a good, clean, industrious woman, who helped the family finances by making silk buttons, while her new husband was considered to be a violent fellow. They lived in a constant state of bickering, and within three months of their marriage Joseph had been hauled before the magistrates accused of assaulting his wife and was fined 40s. Shortly after, Elizabeth was granted a Separation Order, although this does not seem to have been enforced, as they remained living together. In October 1900, Elizabeth once again went to the police to complain about her husband's rough usage of her, and this time he was bound over in the sum of £10 to keep the peace. This did nothing for Joseph's temper and on 3 December 1900, Elizabeth left her husband to move, with her three children, to her mother's house, a one-up-one-down hovel named Folly Cottage in Folly Lane. This tiny property must then have been bursting at the seams, but it is perhaps indicative of the extent to which Elizabeth's marriage had broken down that she was forced to live under such poor circumstances.

Left: *Joseph Arthur Shufflebotham, from a contemporary illustration.* (Author's collection)

Below: *Biddulph Moor church, where Elizabeth Stonier married Joseph Shufflebotham.* (Author's collection)

Meanwhile, Joseph had gone to lodge with his half-brother, Abraham Stanway, at Naylow Bank Farm and on 26 December, presumably in a fit of pique, he had applied to the magistrates for a warrant for the arrest of his wife, on a charge of stealing household articles. In the course of conversation with the assistant magistrate, he had voiced several threats against his wife and when his application for a warrant was turned down, he announced that in that case, he would kill her. Despite his obvious bad temper, no one at the magistrate's office seems to have taken his threats seriously.

At 7 o'clock on the night of Friday 28 December 1900, Elizabeth and her elderly mother, together with Elizabeth's 16-year-old son by her first marriage, Charles Gibson, heard a loud banging at the front door of the hovel, as if someone were attempting to break the door off its hinges. Since Elizabeth had come to live with her mother, the front door was always kept bolted in case Shufflebotham made an unwelcome appearance, and, looking through the window, they could see him pounding on the door, his face a twisted mask of anger.

Elizabeth, fearing for her life, shouted that she would not open the door and begged her husband to go back to his own house, but this only enraged him more and he renewed his assault on the door, shouting that if he were not admitted he would break it down. 'Get off with you,' cried Mrs Stonier, stoutly defending her daughter, 'There's no one wants you here'. Being a well-built, muscular man, it did not take the angry miner long to force an entrance and he now confronted the frightened Elizabeth. Equally frightened and distressed, her mother rushed out into the garden shouting 'Murder!,' followed by Charles Gibson.

Mrs Stonier's 10-year-old nephew, Joseph Rogers, who all this time had been asleep on the sofa, was finally woken by the rumpus and cried out. Shufflebotham shouted to him to go upstairs, but the young boy only went up two or three steps, and left the door open so that he could see something of what went on. He saw Elizabeth lying on the floor, with her husband standing over her and holding something in his hand that the boy thought looked like a razor. He also saw Shufflebotham stamp on his wife and then turn her over. The boy waited, trembling at the desperate struggle that was taking place in the room below, but suddenly everything went quiet and he saw Joseph Shufflebotham go outside into the garden and run off, crying as he went, 'It has done for one, it will do for me.'

Plucking up his courage, the lad crept downstairs into the kitchen where he found Elizabeth lying in a pool of blood and her new-born baby half smothered under her body. Pulling the baby free, he could see that his aunt was still alive and making moaning noises and in a panic he ran out into the street to get help. This arrived in the shape of PC Reynolds, who had been involved in a scuffle with Shufflebotham some weeks before, when the burly miner had severely damaged the policeman's thumb, resulting in a fine of 40s plus costs. Instead of immediately trying to render first aid to the injured woman, PC Reynolds first tried to obtain a statement from her, but soon realised that she was too far gone to tell him anything. Only then did he attempt to staunch the flow of blood from a gaping wound in her neck and in doing so, noticed that the second finger of her right hand was almost severed, obviously damaged when the woman was defending herself. The scene showed that a considerable struggle had taken place, with broken earthenware scattered about, a lamp upturned and smashed and the furniture strewn about in disorder, but in the middle of the room, miraculously still upright, was a small table covered with scraps of food.

Shortly afterwards, Dr Craig from Bradley Green arrived, but he could do nothing and pronounced the woman dead. He pointed out to PC Reynolds that she had a 7in wound in her throat and that death was due to haemorrhage.

Making the front door fast as best they could, the police now turned their attention to a search of the district and Joseph was eventually discovered at Naylow Bank Farm, also the home of his sister, Mrs Beech, bleeding from a wound in the throat. When the police arrived he said that he had first gone to his brother's house, only a few yards from Folly Lane, and in an outbuilding had first of all tried to hang himself and when that failed, had tried to cut his own throat. He also claimed that he had been set upon and had used a knife on the table at Folly Cottage to defend himself. Dr Craig successfully dressed his wound and Shufflebotham was then arrested on a charge of murder. He was weak from loss of blood but was able to say, 'It is a bad job. I left her for dead. I should not have done it, but they provoked me to it. I seized a knife and cut her throat and then did myself. I then placed the child on the sofa and went out. We shall both be better off.'

On the following Monday, an inquest was opened in front of the coroner, Mr T.B. Cull, with Superintendent Dodd of Tunstall appearing for the police and Mr Anderson of Sproston's, solicitors of Newcastle, holding a watching brief on behalf of the deceased's relatives. The coroner warned the court that charges would be brought against the husband in due course, so that for now he would only take sufficient evidence to enable the dead woman to be buried. The jury then proceeded to view the body and visit the scene of the crime, after which Superintendent Dodd said that the infirmary had indicated that Shufflebotham would be fit to be removed from hospital in a few days time. The inquest was therefore adjourned until the following Monday.

On Wednesday, Shufflebotham was taken from the North Staffordshire Infirmary and brought before the magistrates at Newcastle, charged with the wilful murder of his wife. The accused man's throat was wrapped in bandages and he was allowed to have a seat in the dock. For the prosecution, Mr D.W. Eley appeared and elicited from Superintendent Dodd that not long before the crime, the accused had applied to the magistrate's clerk at Leek for a warrant for the arrest of his wife on a charge of stealing household goods, but this was refused. As he left the clerk's office, he was heard to say, 'Very well, then, I'll kill her.' After more evidence was heard, the accused was remanded for trial at Staffordshire Winter Assizes, which began on 15 March 1901 before Mr Justice Phillimore. Mr Plumptre and Mr Vachell appeared for the prosecution, with Mr B.C. Brough defending.

The opening words described Shufflebotham's first marriage to Rebecca Goldstraw, who died on 22 February 1899. Ten months later, he married Elizabeth Gibson, a widow with three children. Evidence would be put before the court of certain acts and threats on the part of the accused towards his second wife and his conversation with the magistrate's clerk at Leek with the chilling threat at the end of it. There followed an account of the forced entrance into Folly Cottage by Shufflebotham and although there had been no actual witness to the fatal attack, there could be no doubt that the accused was responsible. After he left Folly Cottage, Shufflebotham went to the house of a relative, John Shufflebotham, only 90 yards away and there attempted to hang himself in the coalhouse with a washing line, having also attempted to cut himself. None of this did him any serious injury and he then went to Naylow Bank Farm and told his sister that he had been attacked in some way, later being arrested by PC Reynolds who, as he approached the farm, noticed blood on a dry stone wall over which Shufflebotham had climbed.

The next witness was to have been the sister of the deceased, Mrs Emma Rogers, but she was unable to attend through illness. In her absence, a deposition was read to the court describing an occasion about two months before the murder when she saw the accused strike his wife at her mother's house and claim that he wanted the wedding ring off her finger. He threatened to cut the finger off if she would not give up the ring willingly and threatened the life of her then unborn baby, before finally forcing the ring from her.

Hannah Wilshaw, the wife of a stonemason's labourer, gave evidence to the effect that on 14 December, Elizabeth happened to be at her house when Shufflebottom appeared and asked her to go home with him. Elizabeth made some excuse and her husband then asked if she would meet him the next day, to which she replied 'Perhaps,' to which he replied 'Perhaps won't do for me.' He appeared again the following day asking for Elizabeth, and was told that she had gone to her mother's house, to which he replied, 'If I had known she would not have been here tonight, I would have killed her when I was talking to her in the garden,' and added, 'But mark my words Hannah, I will put an end to it and to her.' Hannah seemed to think that most of all he wanted his wife to come home to look after the children.

Another deposition, this time from a fellow miner at the Black Bull Colliery, Rowland Lovatt, was read out describing a conversation he had had with the accused on 26 December, when the prisoner said that he was fond of his wife, but she had been the cause of the breaking up of his home. He also said that he had no peace and would kill his wife.

This was followed by the 76-year-old Mrs Stonier, who described the events of the fatal evening, including the fact that as she rushed through the door to get help, she heard Elizabeth say to her husband, 'Don't, I will come with you.' A bloodstained clasp knife, found at Naylow Bank Farm, was produced, although the accused insisted that he had killed his wife with a table knife.

Next into the witness box was the prisoner, who claimed that an argument started at Folly Cottage, during which he attempted to take the newly-born baby away from his wife, who then punched him on the head several times, knocking him against a screen. He claimed that he was hit several times before he managed to get up again and had no memory of how his wife came to receive her injuries but admitted that he had the knife in his hand when he himself was hit.

Mr Brough, in a somewhat difficult speech for the defence, claimed that the prisoner was fond of his children and that Mrs Shufflebotham was a violent woman with a nasty temper. He submitted that there was no evidence that the prisoner had any animosity to his wife (in fact, no fewer than six witnesses had described threats and some physical violence) and if he had uttered threats, they were merely explosions of temper, which indicated the prisoner's desire to have his wife return to him again.

The judge, in summing up, said that there were three verdicts open to the jury. One was that the accused was insane, but there was no evidence of that, on the other hand, his conduct showed purpose and reasoning. Then they would have to consider murder or manslaughter, if the act was committed under some physical provocation, but reminded the jury that within a few months of his marriage, he had been convicted of an assault on her and a few days later a judicial separation was granted.

The jury took only ten minutes to return a verdict of 'Guilty,' after which the judge donned the black cap and pronounced sentence of death.

Messrs Sword & Sons, solicitors of Hanley, submitted a petition to the Home Secretary for a reprieve, but this was turned down and Shufflebotham faced the hangman at Stafford Gaol on Tuesday 2 April 1901. By nine o'clock, the appointed hour, despite a heavy frost overnight, a large crowd had gathered outside the prison and although in the past it had been customary to ring the prison bell and also the Christ Church bells on such occasions, this was not done this time and the first intimation that the execution had taken place was the hoisting of a black flag. Since the change from public to private executions in 1863, it had been the custom at Stafford to allow newspaper reporters in to view the execution, but on this occasion the High Sheriff decided that this should not be done, much to the annoyance of the press. The *Staffordshire Advertiser* complained, 'We think that it should be an obligation on one of the officials present at the execution to communicate with the press officially such information as may with propriety be made known to the public.'

A Victorian engraving of Stafford Gaol. (Author's collection)

In fact the execution, performed by James and William Billington, had been carried out expeditiously and death, according to Medical Officer Dr Dyer, was 'instantaneous'. It was the first execution at Stafford Gaol for nearly five years and although it was expected that it would be a double hanging, the other participant, Robert Lowe, condemned for the murder of a young girl, was reprieved at the last moment. The *Staffordshire Advertiser* reported that shortly before the execution, Shufflebotham confessed to the Acting Chaplain, Revd R.D. Cheetham, saying 'I killed her with a razor.' By the time James Billington and his son, their work done, had left the prison for the 10.30 a.m. train, the crowd had completely dispersed. At the following inquest, held in the gaol, a juror asked if they could add a rider to the effect that the press should be permitted to attend executions, but the coroner dismissed this, saying that it was all a matter of opinion.

The marriage between Joseph and Elizabeth was a curious one, in trouble from the outset. Presumably Elizabeth must have known that her husband-to-be was a violent man but with three children to look after and little in the way of income, perhaps marriage to a rough miner was preferable to the workhouse. However, the newlyweds must also have considered the fact that upon their wedding there would be ten mouths to feed and within a short time, eleven, which must surely have placed an intolerable burden on their marriage. In the event, their wedlock lasted exactly one year, finishing on the anniversary of its beginning.

4

THE BILLIARD MARKER'S REVENGE

Newcastle-under-Lyme, 1905

On Thursday 28 September 1905, the whole of the Potteries was aghast when the local papers published the dreadful news of the killing of a five-month-old infant in the respectable suburb of Newcastle-under-Lyme.

Francis Evans lived at 40 Wilson Street, Newcastle-under-Lyme, together with his wife Rose Emma, their infant son Francis Walter, born on 30 April 1905, and daughters Emma and Lizzie. They were a hard-working couple, Francis working in the local pit, but as his wife was unable to follow an occupation, having to look after three children, they were finding things hard. In the summer of 1905, they began to think seriously about how they were going to make ends meet, especially now that young Francis had come along. One solution was to take in a lodger and they soon found a likely candidate in 23-year-old William Frederick Edge, whom they had known for about three years and who had lodged with them on and off in the past.

Edge, a short man with a full moustache and a thick head of hair parted in the middle, scratched a precarious living as a billiard marker. He had recently left his lodgings and readily agreed to return to Wilson Street to stay with the Evans' at a rent of 3s 6d per week, on the understanding that he would find his own food. It would seem that his new landlords did not know that he had just left his position of billiard marker at the Grand Hotel, Hanley, and had no money with which to pay his rent. Within a month he was a fortnight in arrears and, having talked the matter over, Francis and Rose, themselves hard-up for cash, decided that Edge would have to go. On 28 September, Rose told him that they could no longer afford to keep him and that he must make alternative arrangements.

Edge took this with seeming equanimity, merely saying to his landlady, 'It does not matter, I have found a position in Stoke. All my people have turned against me and it seems that you are going to as well.' Rose replied, 'We can't do any more for you. We can't help you any longer,' at which the lodger turned round and with a look of hatred on his face spat out, 'I am going, but I am going to have my revenge before I go!'

Right: *William Frederick Edge.*
(Staffordshire Advertiser)

Below: *Wilson Street, Newcastle-
under-Lyme. The murder site
is now a children's playground.*
(Author's collection)

The Grand Hotel, Hanley, where William Frederick Edge was employed as a billiard marker. (Author's collection)

Rose did not seem too upset about this threat and placed the blame firmly on her husband. 'You must not take your revenge out on me, you must take it out on the master, as it's he who says you have to go.' In reply, Edge muttered something under his breath, turned on his heel and went upstairs to pack his few belongings, leaving the house around midday.

At this moment, Edge had no idea where he was going to stay that night and went first of all to the house of his sister, Mrs Selina Titley, and had a short conversation with her, telling her that he was going to look for work and that he might be away for up to two years. When the time came to say goodbye, he rather ominously told his sister that he might never see her again, but she dismissed this, presumably having heard similar statements before.

Edge then return to the Evans's house, where Mrs Evans had promised him lunch for one final time, and he again complained that everyone was against him and repeated his threat, 'I shall have my revenge before I go.' Rose Evans, by now beginning to wish that she had thrown Edge out for good and all, without promising him one last meal, retorted, 'It's no wonder people turn against you, you are too lazy to work and can't keep yourself when you have got it,' implying that money slipped through his fingers, presumably on drink and gambling.

Edge appeared vexed at this and shouted, 'Don't call me idle' but he soon calmed down and when Rose's two daughters, Emma and Lizzie, came home from school, he looked much the same as usual. Having finished the meal that Rose had made for him, he continued to sit in his chair and showed no signs of leaving. Rose went upstairs for a few minutes, leaving Edge with baby Francis, who was asleep on a couch opposite to where Edge was sitting. While upstairs, she heard the child begin to cry.

Lizzie, the eldest daughter, who had not yet departed for afternoon school, shouted up to her mother, 'Shall I bring Francis up to you?' but she was interrupted by Edge who said, 'Never mind, I'll rock baby to sleep.' When Rose came downstairs again, the baby was quiet and Edge was putting his hat on, preparatory to leaving the house. She asked Edge if the baby was asleep and he replied that it was. Without looking too closely, Rose covered the baby with a shawl and went upstairs again, coming back down a few minutes later when she heard the slamming of a door. At the same time, she heard a gurgling sound coming from the baby and going to pick him up she discovered that he was lying in a pool of blood, with his throat cut from ear to ear.

The distraught Rose rushed out into the street screaming for a doctor, although little Francis was by then beyond all human aid. Several neighbours, including Mr Bailey, the owner of a shop across the road, and another neighbour, Mrs Garthwaite, rushed round to see what all the fuss was about and did their best to comfort Rose while someone else went for a policeman, only to find that William Edge had left Rose's house and gone straight round to the police station to give himself up, telling the police that he had murdered a child with a razor, which he produced from his pocket. 'Why did you do it?' asked the somewhat bewildered desk sergeant. 'Out of spite,' was the reply. After consulting with his sergeant, PC Gillies took a statement from Edge, who was then charged with wilful murder before being locked up. On Friday morning, 29 September, he was brought before the magistrates at Newcastle Borough Police Court on a charge of murder. Although to all outward appearances the accused man seemed calm, the close observer would have noticed a certain nervousness about him.

The court was told that Edge had lost both parents at an early age, but had four brothers and sisters, some of whom were in court, and it was noticeable that two women in the public area, each dressed in black, wept continually throughout the hearing. After a brief account of the events of 28 September, Edge was remanded in custody and at the inquest held on the following day, a verdict of 'Wilful murder by William Frederick Edge' was given and he was then committed for trial.

On 9 December 1905, the *Staffordshire Advertiser* carried an account of the trial, held at the Shire Hall, Stafford, in front of Mr Justice Kennedy, with Mr Farrant and Mr Bosanquet prosecuting. Edge had no one to act for him, so at the request of the judge, a lawyer present, Mr H. Staveley Hill MP, agreed to act for the defence. Mr Farrant began by outlining the facts of the case and produced Edge's written statement given to the police, which had been repeated at the subsequent hearing at the Magistrate's Court. The statement contained some allegations about Rose Evans which the prosecutor said might be true or might be untrue (and which Rose Evans denied stoutly) but would serve to indicate that the accused man had a grudge against Mrs Evans and that he had formed the idea in his mind that he would revenge himself on her by murdering the poor innocent child. Under the circumstances, said Farrant, this amounted to murder and nothing else. (The author has not been able to uncover the exact accusations that Edge made against his former landlady, or the reasons for them, but one can perhaps assume that it had something to do with Rose's past history and a possible romantic association with Edge.)

An argument then arose between the judge and the Borough Surveyor, Mr Austin Patterson, who produced a plan of 40 Wilson Street on which he had marked in red the spot where the murder had taken place. The judge questioned this and when he was told the reason for the mark, he said that the plan was not of the slightest assistance to the court and that it was the surveyor's job to mark that which was stable and permanent and not places where he was told something had happened. Looking rather flustered and not a little put out, the surveyor beat a hasty retreat.

It was then Rose Evans's turn to give evidence and, quite naturally, she was in a state of some distress as she was asked to go through the shocking circumstances of her little boy's death again. She confirmed that once Edge fell into arrears with his rent, her husband had insisted that he should be told to go and she repeated the threats that Edge had made to her, including that he had said, 'I shall take it out on Frank.' It was not made clear to the court whether he was referring to the baby, or to his father.

When it came to the details of the murder, Mrs Evans burst into a paroxysm of sobbing and cried out, 'Oh, it's too awful,' whereupon the judge indicated that she should give the rest of her evidence while seated and gave her a few minutes to compose herself. Witness then said that she had heard a door bang and had come downstairs to find that Edge had gone. Going to pick up the baby, she discovered that its head was almost severed from its body. The court heard these words in silence, broken only by Mrs Evans's weeping as she struggled to recount the events of that dreadful day, and it was remarked that at this point Edge appeared to be smiling.

'Were you on friendly terms with the prisoner?' asked the prosecutor. 'Yes,' replied Rose, 'We were like a father and mother to him, both me and my husband.' Counsel for the defence then intervened and pointed out that Mrs Evans had not mentioned before that Edge had told her, 'I will take it out on Frank,' but she insisted that she had indeed mentioned this at the Magistrate's hearing. At this stage, one has to feel sorry for defender Mr Staveley Hill, who can have had little time to take advice from his client, or to read the facts of the case, before the trial started. In addition, the case against his client could hardly have been more open and shut.

The Shire Hall, Stafford, the scene of many trials. (Staffordshire Arts & Museums Service)

Selina Titley, of Enderley Street, Newcastle, was next to give evidence, but it was obvious to those crowded into the courtroom that she was in considerable distress, sobbing bitterly all the while. She said that her brother had shown to her a photograph of their parents and said, 'My mother's gone. My father's gone. I have no home and no money. I have nothing.' She also said that although her brother seemed in a reasonable frame of mind when he first arrived, during the course of their conversation he became very much depressed.

PC Connolly then gave evidence that Edge arrived at the police station, looking as though he had been running, and told him, 'I have killed a child at 40 Wilson Street' and when questioned he had pulled a cut throat razor out of his pocket, which was heavily stained with blood. When charged, the accused man said, 'I did it for spite.'

PC Gillies followed and said that while in custody at Newcastle police station, Edge had made several voluntary statements and alleged that he had been on intimate terms with Rose Evans and that he had wanted to resume that intimacy on the morning of 28 September but Mrs Evans declined his advances. Edge told the policeman, 'I thought I would get my own back. I intended to kill her but I did not get an opportunity. It took me an hour to kill the baby.' (If Edge's words, as relayed by PC Gillies during his evidence, were correct, it is probably safe to assume that Francis Evans had known nothing about the alleged former liaison of his wife with Edge. He would hardly have been likely to admit the billiard marker into his home as a lodger if he had suspected for one minute that his wife's association was anything more than a platonic friendship.)

For a few minutes, the courtroom rocked with excited chatter from the public seats at this scandalous disclosure and the judge had the greatest difficulty in bringing everyone to order. Finally, the thunderous expression on Mr Justice Kennedy's face and a fierce banging of his gavel produced the desired effect and the trial resumed. Dr Morris then described the injuries to the child's throat and said that all the structures of the neck had been severed, except the backbone. Death had been due to exhaustion through loss of blood.

Mr Staveley Hill for the defence, still clutching at any straw he could find, questioned Dr Morris about the question of insanity. 'Could insanity be hereditary?' he asked, to which the doctor replied that it could be. He also agreed that after lying dormant in a person, it might be brought to the surface by some trifling cause. Mr Staveley Hill then told the judge that he intended to raise a defence of insanity and would produce evidence that Eunice Booth, Edge's grandmother, had been confined in the Stafford County Asylum on two occasions, in 1863 and 1866, suffering from acute mania, and had recovered after about three months on each occasion.

The prosecution, in response, called Dr Percy R. Mander, Medical Officer at Stafford Prison, who said that he had seen no signs of insanity in the prisoner while he had been at the prison. 'In fact,' said the doctor, 'he had been quiet and well behaved.'

A written statement from the prisoner was then read out to the court, including that the prisoner had known Mrs Evans for about three years and that he had a great liking for her. He said that he had lost money through betting and gambling and that he had the idea that he would attack Rose Evans and 'finish her off,' but had decided instead to kill the baby. Mr Farrant, for the prosecution, unwilling to let this go unchallenged, said he was instructed that these charges were untrue, but whether true or false, the jury would have no doubt that the accused, having some real or imaginary grievance, formed the idea of revenging himself on Mrs Evans and that this revenge took the form of murdering a poor, innocent child. Such a crime could be nothing but deliberate murder.

Frank Birkin Edge, the accused's brother, said that there was another case of insanity on their mother's side.

In his final speech, Mr Staveley Hill told the jury that it would be idle for him to suggest that the prisoner did not commit this crime, but he asked them to say that at the time of the murder he was insane and not responsible for his actions. He submitted that the catalyst for his breakdown was being given notice to quit his lodgings and claimed that the accused's low spirits and morbid condition on the day of the murder were an indication of this.

In a long summing up, Mr Justice Kennedy dealt at length with the plea of insanity. 'It was very necessary,' he told the jury, 'To be careful in accepting

Stafford Gaol, where William Frederick Edge was executed. (Author's collection)

evidence as to insanity. Mankind was very liable to gusts of passion, due often to causes which had no real existence and which were borne in one's mind either by sudden temper, unreasonable prejudice, or the passion of revenge. This, however, was not insanity but wickedness. Because an act was horrible, the jury must not say that a man was mad. That would be an easy solution of the wickedness of the world.'

It took the jury only five minutes to return a unanimous verdict of 'Guilty' and Edge was sentenced to death, the vicar of Biddulph solemnly saying 'Amen' after the judge's final words. Edge received the sentence calmly and with no apparent emotion and then disappeared below to the cells. His sister, Selina Titley, had to be helped from the court in a state of collapse.

While in gaol awaiting execution, William Frederick Edge maintained a stoic calm, eating his meals with relish and receiving numerous visitors, although his celebration of Christmas Day must have been a grim affair, knowing that he was due to die in two days time. On the afternoon of Tuesday 26 December, Henry Pierrepoint and his assistant, John Ellis, quietly entered Stafford Prison to make their preparations, and at 8. a.m. the following morning William Frederick Edge walked the few yards across an open space to the execution shed with a smile on his lips. Soon afterwards, the usual notices, hung in a black frame and signed by prison governor Lethbridge and the Revd C.T. Rolfe, were posted on the prison gates as the prison bell tolled mournfully, revealing to the small number gathered outside the prison that the law had taken its course.

Wilson Street today shows no sign of where this dreadful crime took place, the houses up to no. 70 having been demolished and replaced by a children's playground.

5

DEATH IN THE GASOMETER

Hednesford Hill, 1919

Henry Joseph Albert Gaskin, a 27-year-old stonemason from Shenstone, a tiny village just a few miles from Tamworth in the south of the county, married Harriett Eliza Poole in October 1890. Harriett was nine years younger than her husband and within days of the wedding, she was pregnant. The baby, a boy, was born on 22 July 1891 and was christened Thomas Henry. He grew up in the village of Hednesford, just north of Cannock, to be a stocky, good-looking young man. However, whatever early promise he may have shown did not last and at the tender age of 12, he appeared before the magistrates and was fined half a crown for assault.

Two years later, he was once more before the beak on a charge of tampering with points on the railway line near Cannock. The fact that this could have resulted in a major accident, possibly leading to loss of life, seems to have escaped him, but the magistrates were determined to bring the matter home to the teenager and fined him £1, a sum that he was completely unable to pay. Father and mother argued in the courtroom as to who would take responsibility for payment of the fine, Henry insisting in a loud, rough voice that he would have nothing to do with it. The situation was only saved by Harriet Eliza, who somehow managed to procure the sum required to appease the magistrates. This gesture from Thomas Henry's mother, who was no stranger to the courts herself, had little or no effect on her son, who was back before the magistrates within three months, accused of the theft of a watch.

This time, the magistrates had had enough and sent him to a reformatory until he reached the age of 19. The fact that his parents were also ordered to pay a maintenance order of 3s a week did not contribute much to the sense of family unity, which over the past few years had become stretched to breaking point. During his stay at the reformatory, his mother again faced the magistrates at Cannock, this time on a charge of assaulting a Mrs Maud Webb, having thrown a bucket of water over her during a row in the street. This resulted in a fine of 14s.

On being discharged from the reformatory in 1910, Gaskin joined the West Yorkshire Regiment on 8 July, but after four months service he was discharged with ignominy for theft and assault. Less than two years later he was again in trouble, accused of demanding money with menaces, for which in April 1912 he was given twelve months in Stafford Gaol.

Almost immediately on coming out of gaol, he married Elizabeth Talbot on 20 July 1913, when he was 21 and she a year younger. It would appear that he had known Elizabeth, or Lizzie as she was generally known, for some time and might even have been living with her before his latest stay at His Majesty's pleasure, as the address for both of them on the marriage certificate was given as 63 St Johns Road, Cannock. Interestingly, the young man's Christian names appear to have been interchangeable, for when he married, the certificate gave his name as Henry Thomas Gaskin.

On 10 December 1913, a child was born, which they named Arthur Henry. Mathematicians might have considered that there was some doubt as to who the baby's father actually was, but Henry Thomas seems to have accepted the child as his own and his name was firmly inserted on the birth certificate.

Marriage seems not to have done anything to persuade Gaskin to go straight, for soon after the ceremony, he began a rampage of minor crimes that resulted in a further appearance at Stafford Quarter Sessions, where he was charged with several counts of burglary and asked for thirteen other offences to be taken into consideration. For this, he was sentenced to three years in Portland Gaol, Dorset.

Lizzie must have thought that she had made a singularly unfortunate marriage as, after all, she had seen little of her husband since their wedding day, although she must have been aware before her marriage that her future husband was not exactly an angel. Naturally, she was lonely; her home life was far from pleasant and she could not rely on her immediate family, most, if not all of whom also regularly favoured the magistrates with their presence. In 1915, Lizzie, who had then been parted from her husband for more than a year, fell pregnant and gave birth to a girl, named Elsie May, on 23 February 1916. This time, the place for the name of the father on the birth certificate was an embarrassing blank. Unfortunately, the little girl did not survive for long and died in early infancy.

The news of the pregnancy and birth must somehow have filtered through to Henry Thomas Gaskin and he made no attempt to return to his wife on release from Portland Gaol in mid-1916, choosing instead to rejoin the army, with the Royal Engineers, who by now were too short of men to be choosy. He was soon in the thick of the Great War, fighting in Flanders, and leave for non-commissioned troops was rare in those days, so it was not until July 1917 that Gaskin was granted seven days leave and arrived home, no doubt somewhat surprised to find that his wife was now living with her mother, Mrs Talbot. That there must have been discord between them cannot be

Left: *Henry Thomas Gaskin.*
(Museum of Cannock Chase)

Below: *The birth certificate of
Elsie May Gaskin. No father's
name is given.* (Crown Copyright)

doubted and on one occasion, Henry is said to have threatened his wife with his service rifle, although he later insisted that it was not loaded. Returning to the front line, Henry now found that his experience as a coal miner was in great demand, and he joined a tunnelling company of the Royal Engineers, a notoriously dangerous job. However, it brought extra pay for the privilege of chancing death underground, smothered by rock falls or the even more dangerous camouflets – small counter-mines set off by the Germans, who were just as busy tunnelling as the Allies were. It was also not unusual for rival gangs of tunnellers to break into each other's diggings and a savage hand-to-hand battle with pick and shovel would then ensue, often in complete darkness. Most certainly, the men of the tunnelling companies were a special breed.

On 6 January 1919, Elizabeth Gaskin bore another child, which she named Uriah, and once again the possibility of Henry being the father could be discounted. When Henry was finally demobbed, about a month later, he found that his wife was still living with her mother at 72 Brindley Heath, Hednesford and, pointedly avoiding her, went straight to his own mother's house at Bridgetown, near Cannock, and found work at the West Cannock colliery. It would appear that to all intents and purposes he had abandoned the marriage, and under the circumstances who could blame him?

However, Lizzie was of a different mind and repeatedly tried to contact her husband, whom she had seen for only seven days in a period of five years, with a view to them taking up co-habitation again. Times were hard, tens of thousands of men had come home from the war expecting a land 'fit for heroes to live in' only to find the reality harshly different. It would have made economic sense for the two of them to pool their meagre resources, and would certainly have been in Lizzie's best interests, but Henry's pride had already been severely battered by the advent of several children who were not his and so far as he knew, their father could still be around and might even be planning to father another!

He made it clear to his wife, in a few short words, that he had no intention of taking up with her again and that so far as he was concerned he would try to get a divorce at the earliest possible moment. He also made it plain that Elizabeth's constant pestering was annoying him.

On Wednesday 19 February 1919, Gaskin met an old friend of his in a public house, the Anglesey Arms, Hednesford, near to where his mother-in-law lived. After several drinks there, they tried another two pubs in search of more refreshment, at the end of which Gaskin handed his companion a note, addressed to Elizabeth, asking her to meet him 'round the Pool, at once – important' and requested that his friend should deliver the note without delay. Lizzie, no doubt hoping that her husband had changed his mind about reconciliation, hurried to meet him and the two were seen on the Rugeley road later that afternoon apparently having an argument. They were walking

The birth certificate for Elizabeth Gaskin's last child – again no father's name is given.
(Crown Copyright)

towards the Pool, a stretch of water situated by the side of the Cannock and Rugeley Colliery offices, from where two men saw them go their separate ways; Henry climbing over a fence into a small wood on the hill, while Lizzie headed off in the opposite direction. Snow was falling at the time.

Lizzie did not arrive back at her mother's house, and towards evening Mrs Talbot became worried and went to the police station to make enquiries. They had heard nothing and were inclined to leave things as they were. The next day, with Lizzie still not having put in an appearance, her mother went to see Gaskin, who told her that he had not seen Lizzie on the Wednesday and had no knowledge of her whereabouts since. On Saturday 22 February, Mrs Talbot received a letter, posted in Birmingham the day before and signed by a 'W. Brooks.' The letter read: 'Lizzie is alright, she is with me now,' adding, 'She will send you some money when we get to London next week.' Mrs Talbot lost no time in taking this letter to the police, making it quite clear that she suspected that her son-in-law was the writer and that it had obviously been written to allay suspicion.

This time, the police were rather more inclined to take her seriously and a posse, headed by Superintendent Morrey and Inspector Woolley, confronted the young miner and accused him outright of murdering his wife. Gaskin stoutly defended himself, protesting that his wife's body had not been found and that she could quite easily, at that very moment, be in the arms of the man who had fathered two of her children. Under the circumstances, this might well have seemed a reasonable theory to Superintendent Morrey and his men, but it did not stop them taking Gaskin to Cannock police station and locking him up for the night on suspicion of causing the death of his wife. Upon searching the prisoner, the police discovered a bloodstained knife in his coat pocket, but Gaskin stubbornly refused to say anything about it, or where the blood had come from.

The following day, having spent the night on an uncomfortable police cell bed, Gaskin sent a message to the Superintendent expressing a wish to make a statement. Written on two and a half sides of lined notepaper, he described how he had met Lizzie by arrangement at about 2 p.m. on 19 February and had gone with her into the wood near the colliery offices. Lizzie entreated him to come home with her, but Gaskin retorted, 'What do you mean by having those bastards while I was away?' Lizzie replied, 'It is your fault, you should have come home to me instead of going to the army.' The argument then continued, Lizzie admitting that the father of her latest child was a soldier, whom she named as Monty Harris, and suggested that Gaskin should go and see him. Possibly the battle-hardened ex-tunneller would have been delighted to do just that, but turned the idea down flat, saying, 'I am not going down Brindley Heath again.' Lizzie now entreated, 'Do come home with me, I'll go to bed with you and you can have what you want.' Gaskin, filled with disgust, refused and Lizzie cried, 'Well if you don't intend to do something to keep me, I shall go back to Monty. He promised to keep me if you wouldn't.' At this, she burst into tears and tried to kiss him, but Gaskin grabbed her round the throat, shouting, 'You're a she-devil of the first water and I'll send you to Hell where you belong.' Lizzie collapsed onto the floor and Henry, by now mad with rage, grabbed her and pulled her further into the wood saying, 'I'm not done with you yet.' Gaskin then began to beat his wife with his fists, and seizing a thick twig off a tree, tried to force it down her throat. Pulling his knife out of his pocket, he then attempted to cut off the woman's clothing, while she gamely tried to struggle to her feet. Dealing her a savage kick under the chin, he knocked her senseless and then launched another venomous attack on her with the knife, after which Lizzie lay still. Panting with the exertion, Gaskin then covered up the bloody remains with the clothing, which he had cut off, and a handful of twigs plucked from the trees around. Whether she was dead or not at that time, Gaskin did not know, nor did he appear to care, for he left the scene and went home, arriving there at about 4.30 p.m. About an hour later, he returned to the wood and dragged the now obviously dead Lizzie to the edge of the trees, where he cut off her head and then tried to sever her left leg. This he could only partly manage, so he dragged the body over to a nearby culvert and dropped it in. The head and clothing he deposited in the local gasometer tank, having climbed a 5ft wall to gain access to it. On Thursday afternoon, he retrieved the remains from the culvert and carried them to the gasworks, where he forced a piece of 2in gas pipe into the body to weigh it down. Throwing the pieces into the water, he said, 'Now you can go to Monty if you like' and left again for home.

The statement, written by Gaskin in his own hand, was signed 'Henry Thomas Gaskin' and was witnessed by Superintendent Morrey. Meanwhile, the police had been searching for the remains of Lizzie Gaskin with no success. Rather surprisingly, they had not been able to find any signs of a struggle in the wood, although if things had happened as Gaskin said they had, there should surely have been ample evidence as Lizzie fought for her life. After completing his statement, Gaskin offered to take the police to where he had disposed of the remains, but not before making an unusual request. 'Inspector, would it be possible for a search to be made without the knowledge of the Hednesford police?' The Inspector, presumably knowing full well that such a request would be impossible, nonetheless indicated to Gaskin that such might be the case and, having questioned the prisoner further, the police set off for Hednesford, where Gaskin took them firstly to the small plantation where he said he had 'done the deed.' Arriving at the culvert, he bent down to pick up a stick, and told Inspector Woolley, 'This is what I put down her throat.' Gaskin then took the policemen to the Victoria Street Gas Works where two large gasometers stood, each surrounded by a high metal framework. Climbing over the 5ft wall on the approach to the far gasometer, Gaskin pointed to the water-filled tank in which the gasometer stood and said in a low voice, 'She's in there. You'll want two drags and two men to pull the drags in opposite directions.'

Then began a most macabre search, taking several hours, at the end of which the badly mutilated body of Elizabeth Gaskin was found, headless and with a number of slashes and wounds which could well have been caused by the knife found in Gaskin's possession. It was another two days before the dead woman's head was recovered.

Henry was again questioned by the police and, realising that it was no use lying any further, admitted that he had met his wife for a second time on the Wednesday afternoon, and Elizabeth had then been most insistent that he should come with her to her mother's house where they could talk over their problems and see if there was some way they could get back together again. Gaskin had once again protested that his wife's constant approaches were annoying him, at which she burst into tears. His temper now well up, Gaskin seized her by the throat and strangled her, carefully hiding the body in the wood before returning a few hours later to try to dismember it. He had been successful in severing the head, using the knife which the police had found, but had more trouble with the limbs. That night he dumped the severed head and clothing in the gasometer tank. The following day, after being questioned by the police, he returned to the wood again where he rammed the gas pipe into the dismembered corpse to weigh it down, before carrying the remains to the gasometer tank where it sank out of sight to join the other ghastly remains.

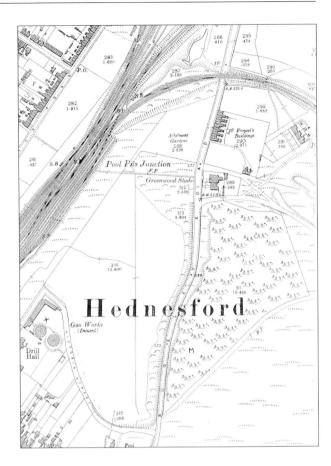

A contemporary map showing the site of the gasometer and 'Gaskin's Wood'. (Museum of Cannock Chase)

The site of 'Gaskin's Wood.' Elizabeth Gaskin's remains were carried across the road in the foreground and dumped in the gasometer. (Author's collection)

The trial was held at Stafford on 4 July 1919, in front of Mr Justice Roche, where Gaskin pleaded 'Not Guilty' to the charge of murder. After evidence for the prosecution had been heard, during which Mr C.F. Vachell told the court that the story of the crime was more full of horrible details than any he had heard since he was called to the bar, defence counsel Mr Graham Milward QC began the difficult job of keeping his client from the gallows. An early witness was Henry Gaskin's mother, Mrs Harriet Williams, who said that when Henry was born, she had suffered a low melancholic state for some four months and that the child had had several fits in his infancy and was always undergoing medical treatment. Henry was sometimes very excitable, she said, and at other times very quiet. He never associated with other boys and on one occasion he had tied a scarf round his neck and nearly strangled himself. It was clear to both judge and jury that the defence was clutching at straws and that these supposed ailments, both of Mrs Williams and her son, could have had little bearing on the actual crime.

To bolster what was clearly shaping up to be a defence of insanity, two Cannock Chase miners, named Woodhall and Dawson, both testified that they had served in the same tunnelling company of the Royal Engineers as the accused man during the war and that they were all buried in a counter-mine explosion at the front line. Gaskin was always reckoned to be a man who took unnecessary risks and he used to leave the trenches to shoot at bottles and to collect souvenirs while under shellfire, actions that led his fellow soldiers to doubt his sanity. The medical officer at Winson Green Prison, Dr William Cassells, said that while under his jurisdiction Gaskin had appeared to be of sound mind, but when pressed had to agree that his war experiences might have affected his mental condition.

The jury, having heard the closing submissions and the judge's final words, in which he agreed that it was a most gruesome catalogue of ferocious and savage cruelty, took only twenty minutes to pronounce the accused man guilty and when asked if he had anything further to say, Gaskin said simply, 'I did not intend to kill her.' A somewhat forlorn appeal for clemency was turned down, the Court of Appeal maintaining that the accused was clearly not insane at the time of the murder, nor was there a case for a reduction of the verdict from guilty of murder to manslaughter.

The governor of Birmingham Prison, where Gaskin was being held, immediately telegraphed to the Home Office requesting a list of competent executioners, and in turn received a note recommending William Willis, 'If an assistant executioner was needed.' The governor then protested that the male population of his prison was 310 and increasing and 'If Gaskin hangs, I cannot carry on without extra assistance.' The Home Office replied promptly, promising him that 'the Governors of Liverpool, Lincoln, Northampton and Shrewsbury Prisons have been instructed to send you 2,2,1 and 1 male officers respectively, on receipt of a telegram for their services.'

Clockwise from above: *The murdered woman, Elizabeth Gaskin; Henry Thomas Gaskin; and the mother of the victim, Mrs Talbot.* (Museum of Cannock Chase)

A contemporary postcard commemorating the murder of Mrs Gaskin. (Museum of Cannock Chase)

Henry Gaskin walked onto the gallows with a firm tread on Friday 8 August 1919. With a body weight of 187lbs he received a drop of 6ft 3in from John Ellis and assistant, William Willis. The Execution Book for Winson Green Prison, held at Birmingham Archives, shows that after the execution, in line with normal practice, Ellis carefully measured the distance from the floor of the scaffold to the heels of the suspended culprit in order to ascertain the stretch of the neck that had taken place. This was usually about 1½in and was so in Gaskin's case. The Execution Book also shows that Gaskin was buried within the prison walls, in an unmarked grave identified only as no. 20. The *Birmingham Gazette* noted that a crowd of some 200 people waited outside the prison and rushed forward to read the two formal notices posted on the gate as the prison bell tolled its mournful note.

Four years later, John Ellis, having resigned his position as executioner, appeared before Rochdale Magistrates Court on a charge of attempted suicide, using an automatic pistol. The Chairman of the Magistrates, knowing full well who the man up before him was, seemed inclined to give Ellis every consideration, saying to him, 'If your aim had been as straight at the drops you have given, it would have been a bad job for you.' Adding that it would be advisable for Ellis to give up the drink, he was discharged. After touring fairgrounds and seaside shows for a time, depression once more took over and, after returning home on Tuesday 20 September 1932, Ellis suddenly produced a razor, and after threatening his wife and daughter, used it to cut his own throat and died immediately.

Files at the National Archives reveal that the day after Gaskin's execution, a stiff letter was sent from the Home Office to the governor of Birmingham Prison, complaining that a letter from the Secretary of State informing the governor that Gaskin's appeal had been turned down had not been acknowledged and demanding that he should explain the reason for this omission. The governor, no doubt smarting under this outburst of red tape, replied immediately, 'It is regretted that owing to an oversight, the letter was not sent. I beg to attach it in case it is still required to complete the papers.' No doubt all parties considered that honour was now satisfied.

6

LETTER FOR A DEAD MAN

Hanley, 1920

Charles Colclough, aged 45, was a fish salesman who lived at 10 Oak Street, Hanley. He was married with two grown up sons and sometimes ran a fish stall on Hanley market, earning between £3 and £4 a week. He had become estranged from his wife due to her drinking habits, although it has to be said that Colclough could more than hold his own in the drinking stakes himself. His parents were potters and he was educated at Hanley council school, leaving at the age of 13 for a succession of poorly paid jobs before going into business on his own.

During his married life, his wife had left him on several occasions due to his cruel treatment of her and in the latter part of 1914 he had enlisted in the 2nd battalion North Staffordshire Regiment, later transferring to the 2nd/7th Highland Light Infantry. He was discharged on 6 April 1919 with his military character stated to be 'indifferent' and from August 1920 he had been living with Annie Shenton, the estranged wife of George Henry Shenton. She had been married to her husband for four years and previous to that she had, for a short time, lived with Colclough and had fled to him again when George Shenton's drinking became unbearable, but this situation changed on Saturday 30 October when, for reasons of her own, Annie decided to go back to her husband, leaving behind her a letter addressed to Colclough, in which she asked him 'not to fly to drink' and asking him to forgive her. 'I feel,' she wrote, 'As if I am going to be ill again and then I would not be able to look after you. I would like you to get a nice place of lodgings, where you would be looked after, as I always wish to see you looking well.'

These tender expressions do not seem to have mollified Colclough's hurt feelings and on the following day at around 4.30 p.m. he went to the Shentons' house at 15 Durham Street, Hanley, to confront the man whose wife had lately been the object of his affections. Although only of moderate height, being about 5ft 5in tall, Colclough was of an athletic and powerful build and could handle himself in a rough and tumble; he also had a number

Oak Street, Hanley. Charles Colclough lived at no. 10. (Author's collection)

of convictions against him for violence. He had received six strokes of the birch for stealing an overcoat in 1889, two months for assault in 1890, six months for drunkenness and assaulting a police officer in 1899 and twenty other summary drunkenness and assault charges. He was obviously not a man much given to forgiveness.

Hammering loudly on the door of the terraced house, he found it unlocked and burst into the hall, shouting that he wanted a reckoning with George Shenton, who at the time was upstairs in bed with his wife. Annie Shenton came downstairs almost immediately to try and persuade her former lover to go home, but he pushed past her, calling loudly for George Shenton to come down and talk to him. Eager to prevent his affairs coming to the attention of his neighbours, Shenton, a big man standing nearly 6ft in height, came downstairs clad only in his shirt and confronted Colclough. They went into the front parlour where voices once more became raised and a furious struggle ensued, watched fearfully by Mrs Shenton, who cowered by the parlour door. The two men closed with one another, knocking over a chair as they did so and dislodging ornaments from the fireplace. Suddenly, Shenton gave a cry and fell to the ground, Colclough leaving the house as quickly as he had entered it.

To her horror, Annie Shenton saw her husband lying in a widening pool of blood with two huge gashes across his throat, a razor lying beside his body, obviously left there by Colclough. Screaming in panic, she dashed out into the street and went to the house of her niece, Annie Oakley, who lived just a few doors away. Annie wasted no time in going for the police, and Police Sergeant Dillon and Constable Tennant soon appeared, to find that Shenton was dead.

Colclough, in the meantime, had run back to his sister's house nearby, where the policemen found him soon afterwards and arrested him, taking him to the police lock-up, where he was charged. Colclough replied, 'I have a perfect answer to that. I did not go to see him; I went to see his wife – with whom I have been cohabiting – with regard to some money and other things that she has taken. They were in bed at the time. I asked them to come down and let us have a fair understanding. I only want my rights. He came downstairs and sprang on me and got me on the floor. I did not know that I had got a razor on me. As I lay on the floor and he lay on top of me, I put my hand in my overcoat pocket and felt a razor. I pulled it out and lost control of myself.'

The following day, Colclough was brought before the magistrates at Hanley Police Court and in front of a packed public gallery was charged with the wilful murder of George Shenton. Colclough appeared to be in control of himself and remained calm throughout the hearing, being represented by Mr P.J. McKnight, a local solicitor.

Chief Inspector Gunston told the hearing that Colclough had appeared outside 15 Durham Street, shouting, 'It's Charlie. Come down, I want a reckoning with you.' Mrs Shenton appeared at the top of the stairs and told him to go away, coming down to try to push him back into the street. Shenton followed her, clad only in his shirt and socks and a struggle ensued, during which the prisoner drew a razor and cut Shenton's throat savagely. Mrs Shenton bravely tried to take hold of her husband's attacker but he shoved her away, saying 'I'll do for you as well, if you don't loose me,' after which he left the house. Chief Inspector Gunston added that there was evidence that Colclough had been drinking, but that he seemed to be quite normal when charged and knew what he was doing. Colclough was then remanded until the following Tuesday.

The next day, 2 November, an inquest was formally opened at Hanley Town Hall in front of the coroner, Mr W.M. Huntbach, and in Colclough's absence, Mr McKnight again represented him. The first witness was Annie Shenton, who appeared in a distressed state and tearfully told the hearing that her husband was so drunk when Colclough arrived that he could not put up much of a struggle and that she did not know how he had managed to get down the stairs. She identified the razor as being one used by Colclough at his own house in Oak Street and said that he was very fond of her and was jealous of her husband. When questioned by Mr McKnight, she said that when her husband came downstairs, he said nothing to Colclough about fighting and she was sure that he did not put his hands up. When the two men fell to the floor, Colclough was on top all the time.

Mr McKnight went on, 'Do you know that he put this razor in his overcoat pocket last Tuesday to take it back to Mrs Peake (the landlady of the Albert Inn), who had lent it to him?' The widow shook her head. 'I don't know that,' she wept. Sensing that Annie Shenton was close to collapse, the coroner leaned forward and said to her kindly, 'Have you any friends who can look after you?,' at which the poor woman burst into tears again and sobbed, 'No, I have not a friend in the world now.' She was allowed to leave the witness box and PC Tennant appeared in her place. He agreed that George Shenton was already dead when he arrived at Durham Street and that Colclough smelled of drink when arrested, although he appeared to be in full possession of his senses. He also agreed that there was a considerable difference in the height and build of the two men and he did not think that Shenton would have stood much chance in a proper stand-up fight with his opponent.

Police Sergeant Bunney, who had assisted in the arrest, had noticed blood on the man's collar, jacket, waistcoat and trousers and also told the court that Colclough had produced the case for the razor from his overcoat pocket while he was being taken to the police station.

Summing up, the coroner said that the evidence was almost as simple as it was painful. They had heard clear evidence that the deceased met his death at the hands of the accused man and he commented particularly that Mrs Shenton had given her evidence fairly and without malice to Colclough. After an absence of only seven minutes, the coroner's jury brought in a verdict of murder against Charles Colclough, who was remanded to the Autumn Assizes at Stafford.

The hearing began on 20 November 1920 before Mr Justice Hugo Joseph Young, where Colclough was represented by Mr Arthur Powell QC. Appearing for the prosecution were Mr C.F. Vachell QC, and Sir Park Goff.

The accused man, dressed in a blue overcoat, walked firmly into the dock and answered, 'Not guilty, sir' when the charge of murder was read to him. Opening the case for the prosecution, Mr Vachell told the jury that he was sure that his learned friends for the defence would direct their efforts to obtaining a verdict of manslaughter, but that while he was anxious to put the case for the Crown without any exaggeration or pressure, he regretted that he would not be able to assist the defence in reducing the crime from murder. He then described how Annie Shenton had left her husband because of his cruelty and his drinking habits and had gone to live with the prisoner in August 1920. She stayed with him until Saturday 30 October when, during his absence and for reasons said to be that she was ill, they were short of money and that no great happiness was in store for them if they stayed together, she decided to return to her husband. Colclough did not return home until around 10 p.m.

that evening, to find a letter from Annie in which she said that she was leaving because her mind had not been at rest since she stopped work and she feared that she was going to be ill again. The letter went on, 'I hope you will forgive me for the step I am taking, as I am only making you miserable as well as myself and you so soon get vexed with me. I think it will be best for us to part and I hope you won't make things worse for me by coming after me.' She hoped that when they met they would be friends and finished, 'your ever-loving wife that should be, Nan.'

The events that followed were described in court; how she had heard a knock on the front door while she and her husband were in bed, and had found Colclough demanding a confrontation. Her husband had appeared at the top of the stairs, dressed only in his shirt and socks and after a short scuffle, Shenton had collapsed to the floor, with the accused man on top of him. The horrified wife tried to pull her husband free, but had not the strength to do it. When at last Colclough made to leave, he had said to her, 'Get out of the road, or I will do you in as well.'

Dr Kingsley, the police surgeon, said that the wound in Shenton's throat was 10in long and cutting clean through to the bone at the back of the neck. It would have taken considerable force to cause a wound of that nature. There was no evidence of alcohol being taken by the dead man prior to the incident. PC Tennant once more confirmed that the dead man was a strapping six-footer and that Colclough would have stood little chance in a fair fight.

Mr Vachell intervened to point out that if every word of Colclough's statement to the police was true, it did not excuse him pulling a razor on an unarmed man.

Mrs Shenton, a small, pale-faced woman, appeared dressed in black, relieved only by a touch of white at the neck. Her husband, she said, used to knock her about and that was why she had left him to live with Colclough. She used to earn 32s per week, but that had stopped, due to a strike. When she decided to go back to her husband, she took with her what little money she had, together with some food that she did not think would be any use to Colclough. There was also a clock, but she had bought that with her own money.

Upon conclusion of the case for the Crown, Colclough went into the witness box and gave his own account. He claimed that he and Mrs Shenton had been living happily together and that he had had no warning that she was thinking of leaving him to return to her husband. The day after she left, he had about five pints of beer before he went to Shenton's house to confront Annie about some money and other items that she had taken away with her, including the sheets from their bed. At that time, he claimed, he did not know that he had the razor in his coat pocket. Shenton had rushed at him and both men fell to the floor. He knew that he had two keys in his coat pocket and it was these keys that he was feeling for as the fight commenced. Instead, he found the razor.

Colclough: 'We rolled over a time or two. Her husband was on top of me and he got me by the throat and was almost strangling me. I suddenly remembered that I had the keys in my pocket and put my hand in my pocket to reach them. I was going to jab him with them. Instead, I pulled out a razor I did not know I had.'

Mr Powell, for the prosecution: 'Was it loose in your pocket?'

Colclough: 'Yes sir.'

Mr Powell: 'What did you do with the razor?'

Colclough: 'On the spur of the moment...'

Mr Powell: 'It was all done on the spur of the moment?'

Colclough: 'Yes sir. I had no quarrel with Mr Shenton and I had nothing to reckon up with him.'

Cross-examined, Colclough admitted that he had not shown any marks on his throat to the police when arrested. Neither did he say anything about the keys. Mrs Shenton's story of the fight was untrue but he could not say why she should have wished to make the case against him blacker than it was.

During his closing speech, Mr Vachell asked the jury if they could doubt that Colclough went to the house with the razor with the intention of wreaking vengeance on George Shenton, whose wife he desired. For the defence, Mr Powell pleaded for a verdict of self-defence. He emphasised that Colclough had no quarrel with George Shenton and that the highest verdict the jury could arrive at would be manslaughter.

Mr Justice Young spoke for just over an hour, pointing out that Colclough's submission was that he had acted in self-defence and that he had not intended to use the razor. It was for the jury to consider why the accused man had said nothing about this to the police when he made his statement or why he had not mentioned the keys.

After half an hour's deliberation, the jury returned a verdict of guilty of wilful murder and the judge pronounced sentence of death. Colclough's only reply was 'I am innocent' and as he turned to go down to the cells, he waved to some people in the public gallery.

A public petition for a reprieve was unsuccessful, even though some 2,700 people signed it, and his counsel raised the question at the Court of Appeal of whether the verdict should have been 'Not Guilty' or 'Manslaughter.' The Appeal judges found that there were no grounds for thinking that there was either non-direction or misdirection by the judge and the appeal was dismissed.

On 30 December, the day before he was due to be executed, the governor of Strangeways Prison sent a telegram to the Home Office with the message that Charles Colclough, under sentence of death, had made a statement saying that 'Although I am going to die on Friday, I did not go to that house with the intention of either fighting or killing the deceased. I did not even know he was there. I simply went to see the woman to get some property which she had taken away with her.'

The Home Office replied that that information was before the jury at the trial and before the Court of Criminal Appeal. There was to be no departure from the decision already made and Colclough was hanged by John Ellis on Friday 31 December 1920 at 8 a.m. The condemned man weighed 119lbs (8½ stone) and was given a rather long drop of 8ft 4in, due to his stocky build. The morning was dark, with rain falling heavily, and few people waited outside Strangeways Prison for the usual notices to be posted. As the prison bell tolled on that dismal and rain-soaked morning, a postman approached the prison gates and asked someone in the small crowd, 'Who are they tolling the bell for?' When told that the man's name was Colclough, he said, 'Hard lines. I've got an express letter for him here!'

7

DID HE DO IT?

Talke, 1921

The small former mining village of Talke, originally Talk-o'-th'-Hill, at the north-western end of the Potteries, has managed to survive to the present day without unduly troubling the world's press, although it did get a mention in July 1782 when a serious fire burned down many of the houses there, and only a month later when nearly two tons of gunpowder blew up while being carted through the village, causing the death of the waggoner, his horses and the destruction of two nearby cottages. The damage resulting from these two incidents totalled nearly £2,400, a monumental sum for the inhabitants to bear, but they were saved by their position coming to the attention of King George III, who arranged for a nationwide collection for the relief of the inhabitants. In 1866, 91 miners were killed in an explosion at Talk-o'-th'-Hill colliery and nine years later tragedy struck again when another pit explosion left 42 mineworkers dead. However, the events of Friday 2 December 1921 were to surpass anything that had gone before in gossip, rumour and press coverage.

The Swan Inn, which still stands today, although much altered inside, occupies a prominent position at the summit of a steep ridge, next to the small parish church of St Martin's. The church has a long history, although the present-day building is relatively modern, and across the road is a Saxon cross. Walter Hulse, the landlord of the Swan in 1921, was a well-to-do businessman who, apart from running the hotel, also had a forty-acre farm and a small milk round. People's opinions of him varied, many thinking him to be an amiable, easygoing man, always ready with a joke and considered to be the ideal publican, while others gritted their teeth whenever they talked of him, maintaining that he was a difficult man and a harsh employer, mean to the point of avarice and quick to take offence. Quite why there should have been such a dichotomy of opinion is unclear, but despite this the Swan was a popular pub, well patronised by the locals and, according to the *Staffordshire Sentinel*, Hulse was a 'highly respectable gentleman and had no enemies.'

Walter Hulse's wife, Mary Jane, was a quiet, unassuming woman who, with the help of her two children, assisted her husband in the running of the busy pub. In the manner of such establishments of the time, those who sought

Above: *The Swan Inn, Talke, 2007.* (Author's collection)

Left: *The Saxon cross, Talke.* (Author's collection)

refreshment there did not confine themselves to the public rooms of the inn, but often overflowed into the kitchen, where there was always a cheery fire burning and a welcoming old settle.

Early on the morning of Friday 2 December 1921, shortly before 4 a.m., Mary Hulse stirred in her sleep, imagining that she had heard a mouse running about the bedroom, but quickly settled down again under the warm covers. Suddenly her husband sat up in bed and shouted out, 'Hello! Who's there?' In the darkness, Mary could hear someone moving in the room and immediately afterwards came the sound of gunshots, seemingly only inches from her head. She felt her husband slump back onto the pillows, and lie there, without making another sound. He had been hit by a shotgun burst directly between the eyes and half his head had been demolished, the wall behind him splattered with blood and brains.

The terrified Mrs Hulse lay for a few seconds, unable to move, and heard the sound of someone running down the stairs, followed by the slamming of the front door. She was covered in her husband's blood and she screamed for help, knowing instinctively that although she could see nothing in the darkened room, her husband was beyond human aid. From the adjoining bedrooms came running her 18-year-old son, Walter junior, together with his sister Cassie May, followed by the live-in maidservant, to give aid to the stricken publican and his hysterical wife. By the guttering light of a taper, it was plain to see that nothing could be done for Hulse senior and young Walter returned to his own room, got dressed and went out into the early morning to fetch assistance.

On his arrival, PC Fred Jones, after taking in the dreadful scene of carnage, spotted the shotgun standing in a recess at the bottom of the stairs leading to the bedrooms. He opened the gun and examined it as well as he could in the dim light. As far as he could tell, the barrels had soot in them and appeared to have been fired recently. Going back upstairs to the bedroom, he made another cursory inspection of the dead publican, noting the main damage and another gunshot wound in the right cheek, about the size of a shilling and then hurried back to the police station to send for Inspector George Williams from Kidsgrove. It was an hour before the Inspector arrived, during which time PC Jones returned and did his best to calm down the still hysterical Mrs Hulse and her two children. On being let in through the front door of the inn, Inspector Williams noticed the shotgun, which lay against the wall and wrinkled his nose at the strong smell of gunpowder in the room. Gingerly, he opened the weapon and saw to his surprise that the spent cartridges had been ejected, although he could find no sign of them on the floor, a strange thing for an escaping murderer to do, he thought, while seeking to escape the scene of his crime. The constable denied all knowledge of the missing items.

In response to questions from Inspector Williams, Mrs Hulse, who was still in a state of shock, told him that her husband had only recently sacked one of his labourers, a 39-year-old man named James Edward Linney, usually known as 'Teddy,' who lived at 129 Crown Bank, Talke, just across the road from the inn. Linney was stone deaf and even his wife and family found the greatest difficulty in carrying a conversation with him. He had actually lived-in at the Swan Hotel for about seven years, but had got married last February and moved out, but he knew the living arrangements of the Hulse family and also where the shotgun was normally kept (standing up by the side of the grandfather clock). Linney also knew that cartridges for the gun were kept in a box in the kitchen sideboard. There was a story going round the village, the stricken woman told the Inspector, that when Linney received his last wages from Walter Hulse they were 7s less than he thought there should have been and a row between the two men had followed. It was this incident, Mrs Hulse said, that had precipitated Linney's dismissal. However, enquiries of some of the neighbours disclosed that in the opinion of the locals, although Linney was difficult to talk to, he was an intelligent and respected man.

The initial reaction of the police was that there seemed to be no motive for the savage attack, unless it was robbery. Mr Hulse was in the habit of keeping his takings in a cashbox, which he carried upstairs each night and placed on a chair by the bed. On the night of the murder, the box had held approximately £20 in notes and silver, none of which was missing. In response to police enquiries over the next few days, there were no reports of any strangers being seen in the village and the police thought the idea that someone would have entered the hotel with the deliberate intention of killing Walter Hulse was unlikely. It was, however, clear that whoever the assailant was, he would have had to know something of the geography of the Swan Inn. The building was old-fashioned and lit by gas, with complicated passages and a winding staircase, and at the time of the murder all the lights were out and the place was in darkness. For this reason, it was equally unlikely that the assailant could have been a stranger.

As dawn broke, the policemen made a search of the outside of the premises and noticed wet earth on the sill of the window to the snug, at the rear of the property, which was also unlatched. Mrs Hulse told the policemen that when Linney lodged with them and came in late, he would often worm his way through the snug window to save rousing the rest of the household. The widow also remembered that while she lay, terrified, beside the body of her murdered husband, she had heard footsteps leaving the room, which she now positively identified as belonging to Linney.

This seemed to be stretching things a bit far, thought Inspector Williams, but Mrs Hulse went on to elaborate – Linney walked with a limp, with a tendency to lean to one side as he moved, and she had known instantly that the retreating footsteps in the darkened bedroom belonged to their former employee. At this stage PC Jones interjected. He had, so he told his Inspector, passed Linney's cottage, which was one of a row of similar properties a short distance from the inn, only fifteen minutes or so before being called to the

Swan and he had seen a 'steady white light' in the front room of the cottage. This piece of evidence on its own proved nothing, of course, although it did tend to show that a member of the Linney family was up and about at that time of the morning.

Things were now looking black for Linney, and by 7.15 a.m. Inspector Williams and the constable were knocking on the door of his cottage. The door was opened by Mrs Ruby Marion Linney, who was considerably younger than her husband, and Inspector Williams straightway asked her if her husband had been out of the house between 3 a.m. and 4 a.m. Mrs Linney denied that he had gone out at all and offered an explanation for the light that PC Jones had seen. Her baby had been unwell, she told the policemen. He had bronchitis and the doctor had told her to keep him warm during the night. Because of this, she and her husband had decided to sleep downstairs, in front of the fire, although she claimed that she had not been able to get a wink of sleep and therefore her husband could not possibly have gone out without her noticing. Linney was then asked if he had any objection to being searched, but nothing untoward was found on his person, although Inspector Williams noticed that the soles of Linney's boots appeared damp. When asked, Linney said that he had gone to the water closet earlier that morning.   After a few more questions, which the policemen found difficult because of Linney's extreme deafness, the policemen left.

Later that morning, a labourer named George Ollerhead was working in the field next door to the row of cottages where the Linney's lived, when he saw Linney come out of the cottage and bend down by a heap of stones. He had a kettle in one hand and, sensing someone near, he turned round and said to Ollerhead, 'What is the matter with the boss?' (meaning Walter Hulse). The labourer indicated that he did not know and then watched as Linney went through the field gate back towards his house.

Meanwhile, Walter Hulse's body still lay at the Swan Inn where Dr W.C. Allardice, Dr McDonald – the police surgeon – and Dr Jones of Talke performed a post-mortem. Dr Allardice said that Hulse had been lying on the side of the bed furthest away from the door. There were pellet marks on the washstand, about 2ft 3in above the level of the bed, and there was a wound in the dead man's cheek, although no sign of blackening of his moustache or face. His head was surrounded by blood and several cartridge wads were found in the room. At 3 o'clock that day, an inquest was opened at the hotel, which was adjourned after evidence of identification had been given.

On Tuesday afternoon, the funeral cortege wound its way the short distance from the Swan Inn to St Martins, where the Revd J.H.L. Edwards conducted the service, which was attended by upwards of a thousand people. Mary Hulse was still too shocked to attend, but her two children were there, together with several members of the immediate family, including Walter Hulse's brother and two sisters. In line with the dead man's position in the local community, members of Audley Urban District Council were present, Mr F. Harrison of Shelton represented Staffordshire Farmers Ltd, and Mr W. Kerr, licensee of another local pub, the Queen's Head, also attended. The service was a simple one and the only hymn sung was *Nearer my God to Thee*. Most of those assembled had been unable to squeeze into the tiny church but afterwards clustered round the open grave in the churchyard, when the coffin was respectfully lowered. A large force of police was on duty in the village, although there was no reported incidence of trouble. A great number of floral tributes were carefully noted in the *Sentinel* and many strangers were seen in the crowd.

Three days later, on the Monday, having now heard all about the murder, George Ollerhead contacted PC Jones and told him about his meeting with Teddy Linney. Jones immediately went round to the field and ferreted about in the pile of stones. There, well down in the pile, he found two shotgun cartridges, which from their appearance could only have been put there recently.

The police now had something to go on, and the following Saturday evening Inspector Williams and PC Jones again visited the Linneys and arrested Teddy on suspicion of the murder of Walter Hulse. So that the stone-deaf Linney could understand, Inspector Williams wrote on a piece of paper, 'You will be arrested on suspicion of murdering Walter Hulse at the Swan Inn, Talke, on the 2nd of December,' after which he was taken to the cells at Newcastle-under-Lyme. Two searches were made of Linney's property, after which the house was locked up and Mrs Linney and her child went to stay with her father, who lived a short distance away.

The police continued to gather such evidence as they could, including several rumours that Linney and his boss had been on bad terms. He had been heard by several people making threats against Hulse, complaining that his late employer had kept back monies owing to him, although Linney had later claimed that these threats were only in exasperation against an employer who was difficult to deal with at the best of times.

Linney was brought before the magistrates at Newcastle on Monday 5 December and charged with wilful murder. Sitting in the dock, he looked round nervously before the proceedings commenced, drumming his fingers on the woodwork. Outside the small courtroom, a large crowd had gathered, most of which did not manage to gain entrance. The work of the court was hampered by Linney's deafness and even when his name was shouted into his ear by a constable, he took no notice. 'I am as deaf as a stone wall,' he told the court.

The magistrates were expecting Mrs Linney to put in an appearance, but word came that she had been delayed by the bad state of the roads, so in order to make sure that the accused man knew exactly what he was accused of, the charge was written down and handed to him. 'You are charged with

St Martin's church, Talke. (Author's collection)

the wilful murder of Walter Hulse, at the Swan Inn, Talke, on 2nd December 1921. You will not be required to make any answer unless you wish, and you will be well advised to make no statement at present unless you wish to do so.' Having read this, Linney, presumably under instruction, said, 'I wish to apply for legal aid.'

The only evidence called was that of Inspector Williams, who gave evidence of the arrest, and Linney was then told that he would be remanded in custody for one week, to give him time to get legal aid. One of his relatives then came forward and told the court that although the accused had some money, it was locked up in War Bonds. He was therefore applying for legal aid under the Poor Prisoner's Defence Act. The magistrate's clerk told him that if Mrs Linney would call at the office, the position would be explained to her. Linney, cap in hand, was then removed to the cells.

The inquest resumed on Monday 12 December, when there was consternation as the coroner, Mr Hugh W. Adams, announced that he had been given information that two members of the jury were related to Linney. It turned out that the Poole brothers were brothers-in-law of the accused man and, at the coroner's request, they stood down from the proceedings, leaving a jury of nine. Linney was notable by his absence and the coroner said that he had been in touch with the governor of Manchester (Strangeways) Prison, who told him that Linney had been informed of his right to be present at the inquest but had declined to be so. Mrs Hulse was now invited to give her evidence and she outlined the events of the night of the murder. She told the court that she had locked up as usual and everything was in order. All the doors and windows were shut. The shotgun that had killed her husband was produced and she said that so far as she knew, it was her husband's. She had never handled it and did not know whether or not the gun was kept loaded. Its usual place was propped up against the clock in the kitchen. The cartridges were kept in the sideboard drawer, a few feet away.

She told the court that Linney had been in her husband's employ for upwards of nine years and that before he married, he had had the run of the house, sleeping in the kitchen. He had been known to use the gun whenever he wished to do so, for the purpose of shooting sparrows. On occasion, the accused would come home late and would gain entrance via the windows in the snug and smoke-room. When asked about Linney's employment, she became a little vague, being unable to say whether or not Linney had been discharged by her husband or whether he had been taken on again as the accused later claimed, although she did admit that Linney's pay had been reduced by 5s a week about three months previously. Asked by Mr Sproston, Linney's solicitor, about this, she said, 'The position was that if the wages would not do, Linney need not come again.' Regarding the footsteps which she described as sounding like Linney's, Sproston asked, 'Having regard to the fact that, on your own admission, when the light was brought, you were still very upset, do you say that at the time you were in a mental attitude to judge whose steps they were?' 'I can only say that they seemed very familiar footsteps to me,' was the unconvincing reply.

Rose Annie Malinda Poole told the court that the accused was her uncle. She had been at his cottage on Friday 2 December, when Linney told her that he had no work to go to, as Hulse had stopped him. The next witness was Linney's next-door neighbour, Rosina Burnip, who said that on Thursday 1 December Linney came in and asked her mother to lend him tuppence to buy a loaf. He said he had no money and was going to a relative's house in Wolstanton to ask her to advance him some money on his War Bonds. He said that he was very upset because if he could not get his job back at the Swan, he did not know how he was going to find work. His former employer had not given him a National Insurance card, or an unemployment card, and that he felt like cutting his own throat. The witness saw Linney later that day and this time he seemed a lot brighter, claiming that Walter Hulse had given him his job back and that he would be starting again on the Monday.

Next to appear was Samuel Hunks Shufflebottom, of Bignall End, who said that on the morning after the murder, at around 7.30 a.m., he had been working at the rear of three houses in Crown Bank, which were known to the locals as 'The Dirty Three.' There was a field adjoining, bounded on the bottom side by a garden. He saw a man in the field, who he later recognised as Linney, in a bending position close to the garden. He confirmed that he had drawn the attention of his fellow worker, George Ollerhead, to this incident. Linney had then stood up, turned towards them and said, 'What's up with the boss?' after which he went back into his house. On the Monday, the two labourers went to PC Jones who heard what they had to say and then went to the spot and, underneath a flat stone, found two used shotgun cartridges.

The inquest dragged on, this was now the end of the third day and it reconvened on the Thursday afternoon. The tiny room was packed to suffocation. Mrs Linney sat beside the solicitor, Mr Sproston. PC Jones entered the witness box and told the jury that he had been on duty at 3.40 a.m. on 2 December, when he passed the Swan Inn. The place was in total darkness but, when passing Linney's house, he saw a very bright light shining in the front downstairs window. The paper blind, he said, although drawn down, was torn.

The coroner, in his summing up, mentioned that immediately before the shots, Walter Hulse had called out 'Hello.' The accused man, Linney, was totally deaf, so he would not have heard the cry and thus it could not be said that he had been startled into pulling the trigger. If a stranger had broken in, it seemed curious that he had picked up the gun, crossed to the drawer to get the cartridges and then gone upstairs, but he (the coroner) did not think there sufficient reason to place the blame on Linney. So far as the light in the window was concerned, Mrs Linney had given an adequate explanation for that. What the jury had to consider, and he pointed out that they were not trying Linney in any way, was who had fired the gun, if they thought the evidence was there for them to say so. At length, the jury were sent out to consider their verdict, which was, 'Murdered by someone unknown.'

The trial began at Stafford on 23 February 1922 before the redoubtable Horace Avory, when Mr Charles Vachell KC again appeared for the prosecution. There had already been a hearing before the Grand Jury, who had found a True Bill against the accused and this was faithfully reported in the *Staffordshire Sentinel*, along with comments that the accused man had, or *thought* he had, some grievance against the deceased and that not long before 2 December he had been heard threatening to shoot the deceased. Such press comments before the trial would nowadays amount to contempt of court.

Two court officials sat in the dock with Linney on Mr Avory's instructions, writing down every word that was said so that the accused man could understand what was going on. An important part of the Crown case was that the intruder seemed to have an intimate knowledge of the layout at the Swan Inn. Not only had he known where to find the shotgun and the cartridges but he had also managed, in pitch darkness, to find his way to the Hulses' bedroom. Linney had actually lived at the inn for a period and so would have been privy to all this information. Ollerhead's story about the cartridge cases was told to the court and things began to look badly for the man in the dock. Things improved slightly when Rosina Burnip gave her evidence and she now disclosed that two or three months prior to the murder, she had seen some children playing with empty cartridges near to the cottages.

Mrs Hulse, in deep mourning, again insisted that the footsteps she had heard on the night of the murder were those of Linney, but no attempt seems to have been made to have the accused walk up and down in the courtroom so that the jury could decide for themselves whether or not his walk was distinctive enough to be recognised in that way.

Robert Fern, the owner of the field where the cartridges were found, said that about three months before the murder he had heard Linney complain about having had 5s stopped out of his wages and threaten to shoot his employer. He said that he had not taken it seriously at the time. Mr Clarkson, for Linney, caused laughter in court by saying, 'I suppose you have heard members of the forces use some pretty rough expressions with regard to Sergeant Majors?' 'Oh, yes,' replied Fern. 'And 99 per cent of them were never meant seriously?' asked Mr Clarkson. 'No,' was the reply.

Inspector Williams told the court that when he visited Linney's house on the day of the murder, the accused man was wearing corduroy trousers. The police had found marks outside the window of the snug at the Swan, which they thought might have been caused by someone trying to enter through the window and in doing so, falling backwards, leaving the imprint of his trousers on the ground, but these marks were of ordinary cloth. According to Linney, he had been wearing the corduroy trousers all week. In the course of re-examination, Williams said that the cartridge cases found under the stones showed no exposure to the weather.

Then it was Teddy Linney's turn to give evidence, first of all taking the oath, after which all the questions were put to him in writing. He repeated his story that Mr Hulse, on the evening of Thursday 1 December, had given him his job back and said that he could start work again on the following Monday. No further evidence of this was available and the court had to make of it what they could, but if it were true, then Linney would have had no motive at all to wish his employer dead. When asked, neither Mrs Hulse nor her son Walter admitted to knowing anything about this. Linney further claimed that the first he had heard about the murder was between 8 a.m. and 9 a.m. on 2 December, having been told about it by a neighbour. He admitted that he had used the gun from time to time and that he knew where it and the cartridges were kept. He also agreed that on one occasion he had come home to the Swan late and had got in through the smoke-room window, which was, however, nowhere near the snug window. He denied ever entering through that one.

Linney was being defended on legal aid and had a local man, Randolph McGregor Clarkson, to look after his interests. Clarkson, aged 33, was eager to build up a reputation for himself, and made a valiant effort on behalf of his client, taking the line that Hulse had been killed by a chance burglar who had fled once the shotgun had been fired. There was no explanation as to why the murderer should have waited to unload the shotgun or why he should have stopped to place the cartridges under the pile of stones but, on the other hand, neither was there an explanation as to how a totally deaf man could have negotiated his way in pitch darkness to the Hulses' bedroom and taken aim. Mrs Linney, in her evidence, had said that like many deaf people, her husband did not know how much noise he made when he moved around, which being clumsy, was quite a lot. She found it difficult to believe that Linney could have moved round the hotel, including struggling through the side window, without calling attention to himself. She also insisted that the whole of the village knew the plan of the Swan and many people would have known where the bedroom was. If Linney had committed the crime, Clarkson pointed out, he would have had to have made his way through the inn, up the stairs, fire the gun, come downstairs again, stop to empty the cartridges from the gun, put the gun in the corner on a tiled floor so that it did not slip and then make his escape, and all the time, he, a deaf man, would have been unable to tell whether or not there were pursuers behind him. Three other people beside Mr and Mrs Hulse were on the premises that night and any one of them could have come after him.

Clarkson also pointed out to the jury the behaviour of the young Walter Hulse immediately after the crime was committed. Confronted with the dreadful death of his father, the young man might have been expected to have put on whatever clothes were necessary and dash out to seek immediate aid, but instead he wasted time by putting on a collar and tie and donning gloves, thus wasting several valuable minutes, with his mother hysterical with shock and grief. Hulse junior had no explanation for his actions: 'it was just what I happened to have done at the time,' he said.

Mr Justice Avory was just about to start his summing up when there was a movement in the jury box and the foreman handed a piece of paper to the judge, saying, 'It contains a question some of the jurors desire should be asked, My Lord.' Avory looked displeased but read the note and then said, testily, 'The question is admissible but I very much doubt its relevance.' He seemed reluctant to proceed with it but then felt that it would be best to get the matter out of the way by recalling Mrs Hulse to the witness box. The question asked was, 'Was the deceased's life insured?'

The answer to that question was yes. In fact, there were two policies on Walter Hulse's life, totalling £512, a not inconsiderable sum at that time, but Horace Avory took pains to warn the jury that no outside intruder could possibly have benefited from such insurance and in order to reinforce the point that he did not think this matter was at all material, he added, 'Nor is there any possible ground for supposing that either the deceased's wife or their son or the daughter could have done this thing.'

The Hulse grave, St Martin's churchyard, Talke. (Author's collection)

While the jury considered their verdict, Linney's companions in the dock filled their time by writing on two separate pieces of paper the words 'Guilty' and 'Not Guilty.' About fifty minutes later, the verdict came – 'Not Guilty' – and Linney walked free. During all the hearings, he had kept his equanimity and accepted the verdict calmly. A Mr George Barber, of Coronation House, Tunstall, met the Linneys outside Shire Hall and took them home in his motorcar. It is not clear who this man was, but the *Sentinel* on 27 February carried a letter from him to the editor, claiming that he had been interested in Linney's defence and announcing 'I have made arrangements that he, his wife and child shall not want for at least a month, during which time I am anxious to get him a place on a farm (where there is a cottage) if possible, away from Crown Bank, Talke.'

Whether this appeal was successful is not recorded and although he had been acquitted, not everyone in the community thought that the verdict was justified. Linney, never the most approachable of people, now felt himself shunned and found it difficult to hold down a job. One day in 1927, he walked out on his wife and family and was never seen again. His wife had stuck by him not only through the trial but afterwards and had borne him two more children after the acquittal. It was thirty-three years before she finally applied for a divorce on the grounds that her husband could be presumed dead.

Walter Hulse lies in the graveyard of St Martin's parish church, next door to the Swan Inn where he spent most of his life. His wife Mary lies in the same grave, with a handsome, five-tier red granite headstone above, lamenting their deaths. Their son Walter junior, who died at the early age of 40, lies nearby. The Swan Inn, somewhat changed from when Walter Hulse ran it, still stands next door to the church but the cottages across the road where the Linney family lived have disappeared under the developer's shovel.

The mystery still remains as to who did kill Walter Hulse. Much of Linney's alibi hangs on whether or not Hulse had reinstated him; if he had, then Linney had no motive whatsoever for the killing. However, there was no evidence to support his claim and no one knew better than Teddy Linney that, with his hearing impediment, he would find it extremely difficult to get another job elsewhere. He had the motive and the means to make a daring entry into the inn, take the shotgun and kill his late employer before stumbling back to his cottage. All this could have been done on the pretext of going to the outside lavatory, but as is the case now, an accused man is presumed innocent until proven guilty, perhaps we should abide by the verdict of the coroner's jury, 'Murdered by someone unknown.'

8

THE BODY UNDER THE FLOORBOARDS

Hanley, 1946

Stanley Sheminant was a tall, fair-haired 28-year-old motor driver, who had married in 1937 but was now separated from his wife, leaving her with two children. Born in Southampton, he had suffered from rheumatic fever at the age of 5, as a result of which he had missed his schooling for three years and now suffered from valvular disease of the heart. He had followed a wandering sort of life, drifting from job to job, before coming to the Potteries in December 1942, where he eventually fell in with a girl named Irene Dunning.

Sheminant had known Irene for about two years and some time ago had proposed marriage to her, but two days before the wedding was due to take place, he had confessed that he was already married, with a family. This does not seem to have put Irene off and they decided to live together, without the bonds of matrimony. The liaison was not without its problems and when her boyfriend began to get rough with her, she asked her friend, Elizabeth Berrisford, who took in lodgers at her tiny terraced house at 6 Cromwell Street, Birches Head, if she could stay with her. Elizabeth, who was separated from her husband and had her 12-year-old daughter living with her, also had a son, Harry, aged 20, who was in the army and away for much of the time. Glad of the extra income, she readily agreed to Irene's request, but within a fortnight Sheminant appeared and asked Irene to take him back. The girl agreed and, presumably with the consent of Elizabeth Berrisford, invited him to share her upstairs bedroom, with the use of kitchen. They continued to lodge at Cromwell Street for the next nine months, during which time Sheminant had a succession of jobs, but did not seem able to keep any of them for long. As a result, and because Sheminant was an inveterate gambler, the couple were always short of money and Irene was prevailed upon by her man to borrow £15 from her uncle, which she did, rather reluctantly. Finding the upstairs bedroom not to their liking, the couple asked Elizabeth Berrisford to let them move downstairs and into the front room, where they slept on what had been Elizabeth's bed. This happy state did not last long as one day, while Elizabeth was out, Sheminant sold it! Thereafter, they slept on a mattress on the floor. Quite what Elizabeth felt when she found out that her bed had been sold without her permission is not recorded, but as she continued to allow the couple to live with her, they must have found some way of pacifying her.

If they had promised to replace the piece of furniture, then Elizabeth was to be disappointed. Her lodgers rarely, if ever, had any money and their rent was paid spasmodically, to say the least. To add insult to injury, Sheminant borrowed £30 from her in November 1945, and Elizabeth had long since given up hope of seeing the money repaid. Her son, Harry, had a bicycle and before long that had disappeared as well; Elizabeth was sure that Sheminant had sold it, but for the sake of her friend Irene, she held her tongue.

On 17 May 1946, Elizabeth had some good news for a change. Harry was coming home on leave and would see her at her place of work in Burslem that afternoon. He arrived promptly, wearing his army uniform, and the two had a joyous reunion until Elizabeth had to return to work. Harry then left, with the intention of going to Cromwell Street. Elizabeth would never see her son alive again.

Harry Berrisford arrived at his home at around 2.30 p.m. and chatted to his mother's lodgers. Irene, sensing that the young man was hungry, offered to cook him a meal, which he immediately accepted, and soon a plateful of eggs and bacon was on the table for him. Some time later, probably around 3.30 p.m., Irene left the house on an errand and the two men carried on talking. Harry decided that he would get out of his army uniform, which was hot and uncomfortable, and went to look for a suit of civilian clothes that his mother kept in the house for him. To his annoyance, he could find no trace of it. Suddenly he had a thought and went out into the backyard. Coming back in, he confronted Sheminant. 'My bike's gone,' he shouted. 'Is it you?' and then having another thought, he asked the lodger what had happened to his missing suit.

By this time, Berrisford was in a filthy temper and Sheminant stuttered that he had been out of work and short of money, so he had pawned it. This made the young soldier even angrier. 'What right had you to do that?' he shouted, and accused the lodger of being a rogue and a thief. Having told Sheminant what he thought of him, he turned his attention to Irene Dunning's character, calling her a prostitute and a bitch.

'What about your mother,' screamed Sheminant in riposte. 'She is the same. You don't know that a man comes here and stays with her!' Speechless with rage, Berrisford launched an attack on the lodger. Standing on the fire grate was a pan of water, now nearly boiling, and Berrisford moved towards it, with a view to throwing it over his adversary, whereupon Sheminant punched the young soldier on the right side of the face and he fell to the floor. Recovering quickly, Berrisford started to get up and clutched at Sheminant, pulling him to the ground where the two men wrestled on the floor. Suddenly, Sheminant

Cromwell Street, Hanley. (Author's collection)

grabbed hold of Berrisford by the hair and slammed his head against the stone surround of the fireplace, where he lay still, a pool of blood slowly spreading across the floor.

Elizabeth Berrisford arrived home at about 8 p.m. and was surprised to find her son absent. In answer to her questions, Irene Dunning, who had returned to the house around 5 p.m., told her that she had made Harry some lunch when he arrived and that later in the afternoon he had put on his haversack and gone out, saying 'Cheerio. I'll be seeing you.' 'Did he say where he was going?' asked Elizabeth, concerned, and Irene answered, 'I think he said he was going to see his girl.'

Sheminant, who had been out when Elizabeth arrived home, came back two hours later, when the three of them had supper. He claimed that he had been out when Harry left and had no idea where he had gone or when he would return. The following day, Elizabeth came home from the early shift at work at about 3.30 p.m. and went to the front upstairs bedroom, which Harry normally occupied when he came home, and found that the bed had not been slept in. Irene Dunning was in the house and looked as though she had been crying.

Over the next few days the atmosphere at Cromwell Street was rather fraught and Sheminant's manner did not improve things. In the kitchen was a baby grand piano, which her lodger suddenly offered to sell, as they were once again short of money. 'That's Harry's piano,' snapped Elizabeth, 'And it stays where it is!' The following Thursday, Elizabeth came home and found the piano missing. Sheminant said that he had sent it to be re-polished and that it would be back the next day. 'See that it is,' muttered Elizabeth, who had noticed that the missing piano appeared to have been replaced by a man's three-piece suit, which lay on the table. The following day, a piano appeared, but it was not the original and relationships between Elizabeth and her lodgers plummeted to a new low. On 27 June, Elizabeth came home and saw Sheminant wearing a pair of khaki trousers, which looked suspiciously like those belonging to her son. 'Take those off,' she screamed, 'Those are Harry's trousers.' Sheminant made a show of remorse and muttered, 'I'm sorry, I won't wear them again.' This episode led Elizabeth to bring up the subject of her missing son again. 'If you had not taken his bike, he would not have left home,' she accused him. The lodger tried to look contrite. 'Why not try putting his picture in the *News of the World*?' he suggested and then offered, 'If you will pay for the repairs, I will get the bike back.'

Elizabeth Berrisford was by now almost at the end of her tether. Her lodgers had stealthily been selling her property behind her back, her son had disappeared and, recently, she had found an item of her underwear among the floor cloths that she kept in the kitchen, covered in blood. Why she had not given her lodgers immediate notice to quit defies conjecture. She was also aware that there was a nasty smell in the house, which she suspected was coming from the front parlour. Her two lodgers were occupying that room, although they were now sleeping upstairs and Sheminant had taken to keeping the door locked when he went out.

At five o'clock the following morning, while it was still dark, Elizabeth crept downstairs and, using a table knife, managed to force the lock on the front room door and let herself in. The smell was now even more noticeable and was certainly coming from this room. Putting on the light and looking round, she saw a square of linoleum in one corner of the room which appeared to have been disturbed and, picking it up, slowly prised up the floorboard which lay underneath it. Holding her breath, she put her hand down into the void under the floor and felt what she imagined to be someone's knee!

At this stage, one is entitled to wonder just what else it would have taken to send Elizabeth Berrisford shrieking out of the house and down to the police station to ask for help. Oddly, she seems to have taken her discovery in her stride and, replacing the floorboard, she pulled the door to so that it locked again and went upstairs to get ready for work. Sheminant and Irene had obviously been woken by the noise of the door being shut and she met them coming down the stairs. 'My word, you're up early this morning,' was all she could find to say.

The next morning, 9 July, at 6.45 a.m., Elizabeth encountered a policeman on her way to work and complained to him that there was a vile smell coming from her front room. She made no mention of what she imagined she had found under the floor, and the policeman thought that he had better things to do than waste time with a woman who could not clean her house properly. When she got home that evening, Elizabeth washed the kitchen floor with disinfectant, but that did nothing to reduce the smell, which was as bad as ever and still emanated from the front room.

It is difficult to understand just what was passing through the woman's head, for it was another ten days before she once more prised open the front room door and, lifting the linoleum, again removed the floorboard and felt beneath it. This time she felt some cloth, and hastily withdrew her hand and replaced the floorboard and linoleum. Another two days went past, and then, while Sheminant was upstairs, Elizabeth motioned to Irene to follow her into the front room where she performed the now familiar routine of removing the linoleum and the floorboard and inserting her hand. This time, she imagined that she could feel a human shoulder. Replacing everything, they left the room quietly and slipped the lock closed again. Irene made no sign that she knew anything about whatever lay under the floor in the front room and her lack of curiosity seems to have been on a level with that of her landlady.

However, the truth was now dawning on Elizabeth, and on 19 July, nearly nine weeks after her son had mysteriously disappeared, she went to the police with her story. At 10.45 a.m. Detective Sergeant George Henry Curran paid a visit to Cromwell Street and wrinkled his nose as the smell hit him on entering the hall. From long experience, he knew very well what the smell was. Following Elizabeth Berrisford into the front room, he went over to the square of linoleum and lifted it, noticing that a floorboard underneath appeared to have been newly nailed down. Once the board was removed, he could see by the light of his torch part of a human leg in an advanced stage of decomposition. Within the hour, Hanley police were on the scene and Sheminant was in police custody, accused of murder.

Detective Sergeant Harold Rimmer, together with Superintendent Till, searched the house. In the front upstairs bedroom they found ten pawn tickets pledged with Messrs George Thompson Ltd, a local pawnbroker, including one relating to a pair of gent's brown shoes, which Mrs Berrisford later recognised as her son's. All had been pledged by Sheminant.

At 4.45 p.m. that day, Detective Superintendent Till accompanied Professor James Webster to the house where the floorboards were lifted, disclosing a decomposed body of a man. Also stuffed under the floor were a khaki battledress, a khaki beret, a haversack, a piece of a cloth belt with buckle attached, a necktie, safety razor, tube of toothpaste, toothbrush, shaving brush, a small canvas bag, a webbing belt and a white towel. Placed over the head of the dead man was a green skirt and a piece of sacking, and round his neck was a piece of cloth belt, tied tightly. The body was wearing trousers, pants, shirt, vest and braces and it was lying on its back, the legs partially bent to get the body into the hole.

Once the body had been photographed and removed to the North Staffordshire Hospital, Professor Webster performed a post-mortem. The body – which was in an advanced state of decomposition – was that of a young man, approximately 20 years old, about 5ft 8in in height and healthy, apart from traces of old pleurisy. The belt round the neck had nothing to do with his death, but had been placed there post-mortem. The cause of death was severe violence applied to the head while the head was lying on a broad, hard surface. There was a wound and an area of bruising on the back of the head and in addition, on the right side of the head, was a fracture which could have been caused by a hammer which Superintendent Till had found in the house. There was no blood on this instrument, neither was any found on another hammer and an axe which were also discovered in the house. Webster did not think that these latter implements had anything to do with the crime. The contents of the stomach showed evidence of egg albumen and the condition of the body was consistent with death occurring between eight and ten weeks earlier. There was no evidence of bruising to the arms or anything to indicate that a struggle had taken place. The skull was slightly thicker than normal and the blows could not have been self-inflicted. Webster thought that the blow to the back of the head was such as to cause a man to fall to the ground but did not think that it could have been caused by coming into contact with the kerbstone of the fireplace in the room.

The usual formalities at the lower court were gone through and Sheminant appeared at Shire Hall, Stafford, on 26 November 1946, before Mr Justice Hilbery. Sheminant's mother, who had travelled up from London, was in the public gallery and the accused man glanced up at her as he entered the dock. He was smartly dressed in a blue suit, with a grey shirt and a blue-striped tie. While the jury were being sworn, counsel for the defence, Mr A. Longland KC objected to one of them, as he knew the accused. Another jury member was hastily sworn in his place.

Mr W.H. Cartwright-Sharp, appearing for the Crown, took the court through the details of the crime, and told the court that the evidence would show that the accused had probably hit the dead man a blow on the back of the head, which had knocked him to the floor. Berrisford's skull had then been smashed with a heavy instrument such as the hammer, shown as Exhibit 15. The prisoner had then taken up the floorboards in the front parlour, cutting out a section of one of the joists, and had buried the body in the space thus formed. He then replaced the floorboards and covered them with the linoleum. From then until the discovery of the body, Sheminant had remained in the house as a lodger and had sometimes slept in the front room, sharing a mattress on the floor with his girlfriend.

One reason for Elizabeth Berrisford's singular lack of curiosity as to the whereabouts of her missing son was explained when counsel told the court that he had been posted missing AWOL by his regiment, and presumably representatives from the military police had visited Cromwell Street and had gone away satisfied that their quarry was not there.

Mrs Berrisford went into the witness box and told the court that when she first went into the front room and felt the knee under the floorboards, she did not realise that it was the knee of a corpse! She claimed that she thought it belonged to somebody still alive, although she had no explanation as to why she had not at once explored further, particularly as the person was most likely to have been her missing son. It had taken nearly nine weeks for the truth to dawn on her!

Sheminant's plea of 'Not Guilty' vanished in smoke when Irene Dunning said in the witness box that he had admitted to her that on the evening of the murder he had killed young Berrisford, saying that the body was underneath the mattress on which they were now both sleeping. She thought at first that her lover was lying but the following morning he told her that he was deadly serious and that she would have to keep her mouth shut otherwise she would be incriminated as well.

As usual, an examination as to the mental capacity of the prisoner had been carried out before the trial and Dr Murdoch, Medical Officer at Walton Gaol, reported that Sheminant was a man of average intelligence, and despite his lack of schooling his knowledge of current affairs was good. The accused man's account of the events surrounding the alleged offence differed from the deposition in some particulars, but it was evident that his memory of all the events was clear. Sheminant claimed that he was subject to outbursts of violence over which he had no control but this did not support the idea that these attacks were due to disease of the mind.

When the time came for Sheminant to give his own evidence, he had no option but to admit that he and Berrisford had quarrelled over the suit that he had pawned. He alleged that the young soldier made to throw a pan of boiling water over him and Sheminant had struck him a violent blow to the side of the head. After he had grabbed the young man by the hair and banged his head, 'All went blank.' When he came to, Berrisford was lying with his head in a pool of blood, but he was still breathing. However, the breathing stopped in a short time and 'I was in such a panic, I think I wiped the blood off and afterwards I covered his head with a sack and a skirt and laid him down under the floorboards.'

Mr Longland, in his final speech for the defence, drew the attention of the jury to the 'dreadful words' used by Berrisford about Irene Dunning. 'Those words, coupled with an attack, entitle you to say that this man was so provoked that a momentary loss of self-control may be excused him,' he told the jury. Plainly, the defence was relying on a charge of manslaughter to save Sheminant from the gallows.

The judge was careful to state that if the jury believed Sheminant's account of what happened at Cromwell Street then they were entitled to return a verdict of manslaughter, and if they thought that all the accused had done was to hit out in self-defence, then he was entitled to walk free. However, he also pointed out that the accused asked the jury to believe that he was in such a state of nervous panic when he found that Berrisford was dead that he was unable to go for help, but instead went through the laborious process of dragging his body into the front room, taking up the linoleum and the floorboards and sawing through a joist to make room for the poor man's head and shoulders. 'A man who said he did all these things in fear and panic felt able to sleep on a mattress on that very floor, within feet of the dead man, and the next day he was able to pawn some of Berrisford's belongings,' he told the jury.

The jury took the hint and were back inside thirty minutes with a guilty verdict. Mr Justice Hilbery passed sentence of death and Sheminant turned to go down to the cells, waving to his grief-stricken mother in the public gallery. On 21 December, the *Staffordshire Advertiser* carried the news that Sheminant's appeal had been dismissed, the Lord Chief Justice, Lord Goddard, not finding it necessary to hear from counsel for the Crown. He made his views quite clear when he said that, 'The crime was a terrible story and a cruel and wicked murder.' Thirteen days later, the *Sentinel* reported that Sheminant had paid the supreme penalty that morning, assisted into the next world by Steve Wade and Harry Allen.

The Execution Book at Winson Green Prison shows that nine years later, on 9 August 1955, the governor of the prison, who had just watched Steve Wade hang Ernest Charles Harding, wrote in his report on the executioner, 'Seems to have defective vision.' No reason was given for this curious remark.

9

CHANCE MEDLEY

Newcastle-under-Lyme, 1948

George Semini was born in Malta in 1924, of respectable parents, his father having been a Superintendent of police there. Although he came from a good home, George was a wild creature and caused his parents considerable pain because of his abnormal ways. He could be very excitable at times, with a marked tendency to lose his emotional balance for very slight causes, especially if anyone criticised his conduct. On one occasion, at the age of 10, he had chased his older brother over the rooftops with an open razor, although fortunately for his sibling, George's anger disappeared as quickly as it had surfaced. A year later, during another paroxysm of rage, he threw a large slab of stone over a bridge on to a small fishing boat, narrowly missing the occupant.

For misdemeanours such as petty pilfering and suspected arson, George spent a portion of his youth in the reformatory, and if these did not cause enough trouble in his neighbourhood, as a lad he had been a member of a gang who, dressed in fancy dress, attempted to stage mock robberies in the Maltese suburb of Ta Xbiex. A neighbour, Mrs Josephine de Bono, complained that as a child, Semini had raided her house on several occasions and would eat anything that he found there, like an animal. On one occasion, he consumed fifteen eggs at a sitting and she was firmly of the opinion that the boy was abnormal. On 1 October 1933 he was found guilty in a junior court of 'leading life in such a manner as might lead to delinquency.'

His parents were driven to distraction as they tried to cure their young son of his criminal ways and they warned him on many occasions that he would end up in prison. George took little or no notice, possibly because he knew that his father would always come to his rescue by paying out large sums of money to protect his own professional reputation and to keep aggrieved neighbours quiet. It was said that young George had tried to commit suicide while in his teens by stabbing himself in the stomach, although this might just have been a product of his fertile imagination; he was prone to exaggeration when boasting about his exploits. One could never be sure about anything that George Semini said and many of his Maltese friends and neighbours used to assume as a matter of course that he was lying. He had been expelled from a number of schools for showing disrespect to his teachers, yet despite this he was not unintelligent and could read and write well.

At the outbreak of the Second World War, George was in the reformatory and was given the opportunity to make amends for his previous bad conduct by joining the RAF. He grasped this opportunity with both hands and served in the Middle East and Tripoli, but after assaulting an officer, apparently for no reason, he was discharged as a mental case. On a previous occasion, he had upset the desk of his Commanding Officer when in such an excited state that it had been necessary to confine him in a straightjacket. Since the RAF now wanted nothing to do with him, he joined the Merchant Navy and when the war ended he came to London, where he worked as a chef. He had left a wife and child in Malta, but showed no inclination to support them, despite frequent requests for maintenance. Later, he became involved with vice, joining a gang involved with prostitution, and served a short term in prison, convicted of inflicting grievous bodily harm on a woman.

His criminal tendencies continued to surface and on 3 January he was fined one guinea at Skegness for possessing a firearm without a certificate. Finally, even London became too hot for him and he fled north to the Potteries, where he was not known. In July 1947, he volunteered to work in the coalmines and lodged in a miner's hostel at Knutton, but by December that year he was in gaol again, doing eight months for inflicting grievous bodily harm.

George Semini was, by any standards, a volatile and dangerous young man; a man with whom it was advisable to be very careful. He practised bodybuilding and liked to have his photograph taken in poses that showed off his physique and had also persuaded a friend to take his picture dressed like a gangster, wearing a large trilby hat, cigarette dangling from one corner of his moustachioed lips and holding a knife in a suggestive manner. Later, he was to regret having had this picture taken and sought to persuade everybody that he was merely dressing up for a theatrical performance.

Little or nothing of his criminal past was known to what few friends Semini had in the Potteries, including the fact that he was wanted by the police for stabbing a man several times in the back earlier in the year in the West End of London, probably the same incident that had prompted him to leave the capital and head for quieter pastures.

On the evening of 8 October 1948, 22-year-old Joseph Gibbons, an electric welder from Liverpool, was out on the town with three of his friends. For the past two months, he had been working as a labourer for the West Piling Company, Stafford, on extensions to the Stafford Gasworks and was living at Frobisher Hall Hostel, Swynnerton. By early evening, the friends had each drunk seven or eight pints of beer and at around 10 p.m. they were in Church Street, Newcastle-under-Lyme, standing outside the Talbot Hotel. Next door to the Talbot was a building which bore the sign 'Assembly Hall' and was, in fact, the local dance hall which was very popular with the young people

George Semini's infamous 'gangster' photograph. (National Archives)

of the district, especially at weekends. While Gibbons and his friends stood near the entrance to the Assembly Hall, George Semini walked past them with his girlfriend, Miss Marjorie Stella Seabridge, an assistant in a local store, who, at 6ft tall, towered over Semini. She had met her 'boy-friend' two years previously while on holiday, and had lost touch with him, but out of the blue, she met up with him again on 3 October and since then had been seeing him every night. One of Gibbons's companions, Frederick Robert Woodyatt, ignoring the fact that Semini was a well-built man who looked as though he could handle himself, shouted out, 'Blimey! She's a big 'un.' (Later, Semini was to claim that what Woodyatt had really said was 'She's a big bag,' slang for whore.) The couple walked on for a few paces and then stopped. Semini turned back and confronted Woodyatt. 'What's that you said?'

'What's it to you,' retorted Woodyatt, no doubt feeling brave under the effects of the beer he had drunk that day.

'The lady happens to be my fiancé,' Semini replied slowly, in a voice that, if Woodyatt had been sober, might have persuaded him to back off.

Woodyatt passed an offensive remark and laughed at Semini, whereupon the Maltese, now in a very aggressive mood, hit Woodyatt in the face, knocking him into the middle of the road. Gibbons came to his pal's assistance and Charles Stanley, another of his companions, tried to separate the struggling men, but other bystanders now joined in the mêlée and Gibbons was struck in the face while attempting to jump on Semini's back. Semini cried, 'I'll get the two of you' and rushed towards them. Within seconds, Woodyatt and Stanley were clutching minor knife wounds and Gibbons was lying on the pavement clutching his left side, from which blood was pouring. In the confusion, Semini coolly turned on his heel and ran off across some spare ground at the rear of St Giles's church while his girlfriend, perhaps thinking that she was well out of it, quietly walked off towards home. The police were called and the three wounded men were taken to hospital, where, after Dr Jean Mary Dance had tried to staunch the blood from a knife wound for half an hour, Gibbons died. The post-mortem showed that he had been stabbed with a dagger or sheath knife, which had passed into the chest between the sixth and seventh ribs, transfixing the left lung and the heart.

Witnesses were sought and a man came forward to tell the police that he believed he knew the man responsible. Shortly afterwards, Semini was arrested at the miner's hostel by Inspector Wright and Sergeant Rutter but flatly denied that he was responsible, insisting that he had been nowhere near the scene of the fight that evening. He said that he had been to the cinema with two Maltese friends, Griscti and Borg, and on coming out of the cinema he had caught a bus to Knutton, where the police found him. He was taken to Newcastle police station and examined by a doctor, but no marks of violence were found on his body.

Griscti and Borg were traced and both men agreed that Semini had been with them the whole evening. If their story were true, then Semini could not be responsible for the killing, but Inspector Wright suspected that Griscti and Borg were not telling the truth and had them both taken to the police station, to be held for further interview. This took place at 5 a.m., when the two men agreed that they had been lying and that Semini had asked them to provide him with an alibi. He had also told them that he had stabbed someone.

The police managed to trace Miss Seabridge at her home in Wolstanton, who told them that she had been in Church Street that evening and that her companion, George Semini, had got involved with 'some trouble.' She had been to the cinema with Semini and two of his friends, but afterwards, the friends (presumably Griscti and Borg) had left them by the Angel public house in Hanley and she and George had caught a bus to Newcastle. She was

The Talbot Hotel, Newcastle-under-Lyme, where George Semini assaulted Joseph Gibbons, c. 1948. (Author's collection)

The Talbot Hotel in 2007, now Zeera's restaurant and The Shalimar. (Author's collection)

insistent that Semini had not had a drink all evening. 'I am fond of him,' she told the police, 'And I believe he is very fond of me.'

Early on the morning of 9 October, Semini made a statement to the police, as follows:

> I was walking past the Talbot with Marjorie at around five past ten. There were some men outside. As we passed, a man made an insulting remark. He said, 'She's a big bag.' I turned back to the man and asked him to repeat what he had said. 'What's it got to do with you?' he replied. 'She happens to be my fiancé' I said. 'So f****** what,' he said. Then I struck him. Two or three more men set about me and I started lashing out. A lot of people started coming my way, so I ran. I had a bunch of keys that I waved about.

Semini made no mention of having used a knife, but later in the day he asked the police if one had been found. At this stage, the police had not made any mention of a weapon and they listened carefully to what the prisoner had to say next. 'I used to carry a knife on my belt, but I don't remember using it last night. I don't know where it is. I must have thrown it away in a frenzy. I told you it was a bunch of keys in my hand, but it must have been a knife.' Semini's room at the hostel was searched but no knife was found, although the police did find the 'gangster' photograph in which he was holding the knife in question. He was now charged with murder, to which he replied, 'I didn't' and that evening the *Liverpool Echo* carried the headline, 'I Do Not Know' when describing the incident.

An inquest was held by the Stoke-on-Trent coroner, Mr Huntbach, during which Superintendent C.G. Nixon reported that a man was in custody on a charge of murder. Joseph Gibbons's father, Thomas Gibbons, told the court that his son had been a healthy man and had just completed his army service. He insisted that his son was of a peaceable and genial disposition and not given to quarrelling. The Superintendent requested a further remand for a week, saying that enquiries were not yet complete and that it would be necessary for the Chief Constable of Staffordshire, Colonel Sir Herbert P. Hunter, to communicate with the director of public prosecutions. Semini was remanded for another week and continued to see the Catholic priest on a daily basis and received the sacrament on Sunday. Ten cigarettes per day were provided 'at the public expense.'

On 20 November, an identification parade was held and nine people, including Semini, stood in the line, the accused man choosing to stand four from the left. Patrick Joseph Carroll and Arthur Ashton, two young men who had been in the crowd outside the Talbot Hotel on 8 October, identified him. Further remands were sought until he eventually appeared at the Staffordshire Assizes, which began in late November, before Mr Justice Hallett. The judge had two murder trials to sit through, the first being that of 29-year-old Mrs

Doris Hales, who had struck her mother-in-law on the head with an iron bar seven times, killing her instantly. She was found not guilty of murder, but guilty of manslaughter, with a strong recommendation to mercy and was given seven years imprisonment. If Semini ever got to hear about this, it perhaps raised his spirits and his hopes somewhat.

After a fresh jury had been sworn, Semini was put up to stand trial for murder. Opening the case for the Crown, Mr Eric Sachs QC, recounted the story of the night of 8 October, telling the court that it was not easy to reconstruct the events of the confused mêlée that had taken place, but it was alleged that in just a few seconds, Semini had wounded Gibbons and his two companions and had then quickly made off. One of the first prosecution witnesses was a Hungarian press photographer, Charles Barany, who also lived at the Knutton hostel, who said that Semini had asked him to take the 'gangster' photograph. The Maltese had taken the knife from his locker and had posed with it, claiming that he wanted the picture for a newspaper competition. Cross-examined, Barany said that Semini had told him that he might be able to get a job in the films if the photograph was good enough.

Charles Stanley gave his version of the scuffle, during which he said that the accused had dropped one arm to his side. When he brought it up, he had a knife in his hand and said, 'I will get two of them.' Stanley tried to back off but someone pulled him to the ground from behind and the next thing he knew, he felt the knife go into his right leg. Frederick Woodyatt said that he had received a knife wound in the shoulder.

When it came time for Semini to give evidence, he told the court that he had served in the RAF and had been discharged because of mental blackouts. There was also a history of mental illness in his family. He claimed that when Woodyatt made the insulting remark to Miss Seabridge, he had used an open hand to push his face, whereupon Woodyatt slipped off the pavement. 'I turned to go away and next thing, someone was kicking me here and pulling me there and my idea was to get away as fast as I could,' he said.

Semini claimed not to remember the actual circumstances of the stabbing. 'I can't say. It is all in a haze. I can't remember drawing a knife. I remember being held back by two persons.'

In answer to a question from the judge, he said that he sometimes carried the knife strapped to his belt, but he was not wearing the belt that night. The knife might have been strapped to his braces.

Miss Seabridge was called to give her evidence and said that she did not hear anyone call her a 'bag' on the fatal evening, although she did hear one of Gibbons's companions refer to her size. She was accustomed to people making remarks about her height and did not take offence or regard it as reflecting on her moral character.

In his final address for the defence, Mr W.H. Cartwright-Sharp QC, made no attempt to deny that Gibbons had died from a stab wound inflicted by the prisoner, but maintained that he had been acting in self-defence. Alternatively, the jury were asked to consider a verdict of manslaughter on the grounds of provocation, or that the blows had been inflicted during a 'chance medley.'

This ancient verdict was originally used in murder cases where the killing did not involve premeditated malice (as in a sudden fight), but where it was thought that the killer was at least partially at fault. In the late seventeenth century it was mostly used in cases of death caused by accidents such as being run over by a cart or a gun going off unintentionally, in order to indicate that the defendant was not entirely at fault. Other defendants in similar circumstances could be found 'Not Guilty' by virtue of accidental death. By the eighteenth century, the verdict of chance medley was used to indicate that although the defendant was at fault, he or she did not have any evil intention. The verdict was, however, rarely used in modern times, and those involved in similar circumstances were more likely to be convicted of manslaughter. In this case, the defence was clutching at straws, as the judge made clear in his summing up.

Mr Justice Hallett left it open to the jury to bring in one of three verdicts. 'Not Guilty' if they thought that the prisoner had acted in self-defence, 'Manslaughter' if they thought that the prisoner was so excited that he lost his self-control and behaved in a way which any reasonable man so provoked would have behaved, and 'Murder' if they thought that the prisoner used the knife with intent to kill or do grievous bodily harm. Chance medley, he explained to the court, was an outdated term that had no place in a modern trial. He believed it to refer to a time when gentlemen habitually carried swords.

The jury returned with a verdict of murder, adding a rider that they thought that an examination should be made of Semini's mental state. Justice Hallett said that no evidence whatsoever had been given upon which they could have returned a verdict of guilty but insane, but the jury could add their rider 'for the purposes of assisting those who have to consider what ultimately should be done.' He went on to assure the jury that in all cases where there was the slightest reason to think it necessary, such an examination invariably took place anyway.

A note in a Home Office file at the National Archives agrees; 'Although the question of insanity was not mentioned during the trial, I think it desirable that there should be a statutory medical enquiry into the prisoner's mental condition. Such an enquiry has been made almost inevitable in view of the assurance given by the trial judge to the jury when they added a recommendation that there should be an enquiry into the mental state of the accused.'

While the defence were planning an appeal, a commission was set up to enquire into Semini's mental state, consisting of Sir Norwood East, formerly Medical Commissioner at His Majesty's Prisons, Dr J.S. Hopwood,

Medical Superintendent of Broadmoor Criminal Lunatic Asylum, and Dr H.T.P. Young, director of Medical Services, HM Prisons. This body visited Liverpool Prison on 28 and 29 December 1948 to examine Semini and the general impression that the convicted man left with the commissioners was that he was a braggart who boasted of his success with women and talked about them. In other matters he was boastful, but at the same time full of self-pity. The Commission considered that although Semini had shown no aggressiveness in prison, he would be easily roused to anger and violence. (Quite how they came to this conclusion is not clear.) They considered him to be of average or above average intelligence and at heart they thought that he was a coward. None of the three thought that he was insane. Almost as an afterthought, they added that they did not think that the old wound in his abdomen was as a result of an attempt at suicide and finished, 'He is a violent-tempered, aggressive man but not a psychopathic personality.' (Letter from the Commissioners to Mr Justice Hallett.)

On 11 January 1949, Lord Goddard gave the reasons for the dismissal of Semini's appeal, which had been based on misdirection of the jury and on the grounds of chance medley. The Lord Chief Justice dismissed the latter reason, saying that chance medley was excusable but not justifiable homicide, and that it no longer had a place in law. Semini had no excuse for drawing a lethal weapon and it was a cowardly act of revenge. Ten days later, leave to appeal to the House of Lords was refused and the *Evening News* on 12 January carried a paragraph stating that the execution was now fixed for Thursday 27 January.

There now followed a perfect torrent of letters to the Home Secretary, Mr Chuter Ede, including one from the deputy governor of Liverpool Prison saying, 'I beg to report that Semini has made a statement to an officer of the prison that, "If I am hanged, my friends will carry out a vendetta against the prosecution witnesses until all are killed." I am unable to assess whether the prisoner has any grounds for this statement or whether this is merely the result of his bombastic nature. The Principal Medical Officer is equally in doubt as to whether the man is serious or not.'

After consultation with the Prison Commissioner's Office, the police at Newcastle-under-Lyme were informed of the man's statement. (It should be noted that any statement or letter written by a condemned criminal was automatically sent to the Home Office, in case it should have any bearing on the case.)

Advocate A. Magri wrote from Malta, enclosing a petition for Semini's reprieve with the signatures of over 14,500 people. It rests today at the National Archives; strips of paper containing the signatures, pasted onto A4 sheets, some in ink and others in pencil, and includes the signatures of at least one bishop, other high dignitaries of the Roman Catholic Church in Malta, all the parish priests, members of the Maltese police force, members of the Legislative Assembly, members of the Chamber of Advocates, medical practitioners and persons from all walks of life. It seemed as though the whole of Malta had united to save their recalcitrant son.

There were even letters from the prime minister of Malta, Mr P. Boffa, who wrote pleading for a reprieve. A telegram from Sir F. Douglas on behalf of the Maltese prime minister pleaded, 'Convinced that Semini unbalanced mind. Strongly urge Home Secretary be asked to reconsider decision not to recommend reprieve.'

This was followed by a further letter suggesting that the jury had wanted to bring in a verdict of 'Guilty but insane' but had been prevented from doing so by Mr Justice Hallett. The Home Office speedily disabused Mr Boffa of his misunderstanding and finally, on 21 January, the Archbishop of Westminster, Cardinal Griffin, added his voice to those seeking a reprieve for Semini. Whatever his faults, Semini's defence team had certainly been able to muster some formidable support for their cause.

None of these letters, however, had any effect on the Home Secretary and there was to be no reprieve. *The Star*, on 13 January 1949 protested, 'If murderers must hang, at least let the Home Office end this ghastly business of allowing them to linger weeks in mental torture. No execution date should be fixed before the question of any reprieve and any legal complications be disposed of.' (The original execution date, 12 January, had been postponed while Semini's appeal was heard and there was then a further delay while the Court of Appeal published its reasons for turning down the appeal – an unusual circumstance which caused much comment in the press at the time.)

Semini himself, while in prison, busied himself writing letters. He wrote to his brother, Victor G. Semini, who was then a police officer in Malta:

My dear brother,
I received your most welcome letter yesterday and though I was grieved to hear how dad took it, and how much pain and worry I must have caused to all concerned, I am glad that you, my people, see things in a true light and as they are, as God is my judge, I swear to you that I did not know what actually happened and I am still at a loss now… You know, all of you, that in my heart I am not wicked and I have never borne malice, even to those who have wronged me where it hurts most. I have been in some tight spots in my life but none can be tighter or more terrible than this. We are all born to die, all of us eventually, but not like this when you know where, when and how… You have asked me to write to the boy's mother. I have wanted to do so for some time but I know not her address. However I will write to the Governor and ask him to forward it.

Victor replied: 'We really should take most of the blame because, knowing you so well, we should have had you cured by an eminent physichiatrist' [*sic*].

Shortly afterwards, Semini wrote to his victim's mother:

Dear Madam,

My eyes are dim with tears and my hand trembles as I take pen and paper and try to put my thoughts into writing... Before I go, I would like to beg on my knees for your forgiveness, please, please forgive. When this happened, I did not know your son and I did not know what I was doing. It was not my hand but the hand of fate. I know how you suffered and how you missed your son at Christmas and New Year, but I too am somebody's son and you can imagine how my parents suffered too... So now, dear madam, I throw myself at your mercy, the law must take its course but I want to save my soul and have a clear conscience again so I beg you, as somebody's son and as a man to please forgive. I had no grudge, no fight with Joseph, it was all a horrible mistake. Before I finish off, I want to emphasise the fact that I did not mean to do this and I beg for your forgiveness and the forgiveness of all your family.

I remain, Madam,

Your son in misfortune,

G. Semini

In all the circumstances, this was a most remarkable letter. Mrs Gibbons replied in a letter that was given to Semini just before his execution, in which she said, 'I will pray for you.'

A few days before the execution date, Semini wrote again to his brother:

Not one officer in the prison thinks I deserve what I got... They painted me as a real bad specimen... They tried to put all sorts of thrumped [*sic*] up charges against me, I can even say that they had people committing perjury to railroad me to the gallows, but I forgive them all and leave everything in the hands of God Almighty.

Your kid brother, George

The date of the execution drew nearer and one final telegram was sent to the Home Secretary, from the well-known and wealthy campaigner against the death penalty, Mrs Violet Van der Elst. Her Rolls-Royce motorcar was invariably seen outside the prison gates on the morning of an execution, with a loudhailer fixed to the roof, which played *Abide with Me* and *Nearer My God To Thee* and other suitable hymns. The telegram read:

The Maltese will be hanged if you do not do something to stop it. The world is still horrified that you let a mad woman be hanged. [This possibly refers to the execution of lesbian Margaret Allen, hanged on 12 January 1949 for the murder of Nancy Ellen Chadwick in Rawtenstall, Lancashire.] Women should never be hanged. This is terrible. More men are being hanged every week. I must let the world know of this. You told lies in the House.

Violet Van der Elst

Mrs Van der Elst may have been a wealthy lady and may have been sincere in her campaign, but the rather frantic tenor of her message to Mr Chuter Ede perhaps hinted at an underlying eccentricity and was studiously ignored by the Home Secretary.

Another letter from a Mr James W– read as follows:

> I should like to be the executioner and that murderer who as got to be executed next Tuesday at Liverpool Prison I should like to be there to fasten is hands behind him and to put the rope on is neck so would you be kind enough to let me no how I should go about it. I would have informed you sooner if I had known. [*Spelling and punctuation as written.*]

Junior counsel for Semini, W. Brian Gibbins, seems to have made a late effort to secure a reprieve, as he wrote a letter to the Home Office on 22 December which referred to a document put in evidence saying that the accused man had been found unfit for further military service in the Air Force by a medical board and that he had a psychopathic neurosis. He also said that the Commissioner General for Malta had told him that Semini was of a highly excitable disposition, with a marked tendency to lose his temper for very slight cause and that when the accused became excited in that way, he appeared to be irrational and to lose his power of co-ordinated speech and thought. Gibbins also commented on the fact that three of Semini's family had been certified insane. The letter was ineffective in persuading the Home Secretary to change his mind.

At 9 a.m. on Thursday 27 January 1949, the meagre crowd outside Liverpool (Walton) Gaol strained to hear the banging of the trap doors as George Semini met his maker at the hands of Albert Pierrepoint and Harry Allen. It is unlikely that Semini heard Mrs Van der Elst's loudspeakers as he fell 6ft to his death.

Perhaps the lives of both Gibbons and Semini might have been saved if a warning issued two years before had been heeded. On the 'Letters' page of the *Sentinel*, dated 19 May 1946, a letter from Mabel Champ, who gave her address as 'Talbot Ballroom,' Newcastle, read:

> Saturday night rowdyism at the Municipal Hall, Newcastle, dances would be readily eliminated if only the promoters paid a little more attention to the entrance door and a little less to the cash desk.
>
> To talk of 'fisticuffs' and fear of 'riots' show an appalling lack of knowledge essential to the smooth running of a public dance; and if I could not conduct my business properly, I certainly should not expect the police to do it for me. An efficient staff, capable of using tact and discretion, but also ready to exercise an unhesitatingly firm hand if necessary, combined with strict supervision on door and dance floor, will eliminate rowdyism and disturbances most effectively, as I have proved during six years of dealing with an extremely mixed and 'difficult' patronage.

The Prison Commission file, made available for the first time to this author under the Freedom of Information Act, includes a letter from Mrs Stella Semini and her daughter Freada dated 24 July 1955. Addressed to The Governor, HM Prison, Walton, Liverpool, it reads:

> As the wife of a man who met an untimely and tragic death and mother of an only child who is now nine years old, I feel in duty bound to bring to the notice of the authorities that since the death of my husband, I and my daughter have been living on charity given by persons who, before I became a widow and had a husband to look after the family, knew our family well and were therefore in a position to judge that the hardships through which I and my daughter have been passing due solely to tragic circumstances over which we had no control and are therefore wholly undeserved. I therefore submit my position for financial aid which the British Authorities may, in their kindness, be willing to grant to me and my daughter on compassionate grounds.

The response from the authorities was a rather embarrassed 'No.' Someone has written on the file 'No authority to grant the wife and daughter of an executed prisoner any financial assistance, and especially as she is in Malta.'

10

ROBBERY WITH VIOLENCE

Barlaston, 1952

The pottery firm of Wiltshaw & Robinson, late of Copeland Street, Stoke-on-Trent, was long noted for its brightly coloured wares, usually marketed under the title of Carlton Ware. Much sought after by collectors, some pieces today can fetch prices many times higher than they were originally sold for in the retail market, although the company actually closed a few years ago when tastes changed and people no longer wanted highly decorated tea sets or colourful vases. In 1952, the Governing Director of the company and son of the founder was 62-year-old Frederick Cuthbert Wiltshaw and Carlton Ware was at the height of its fame, known and respected the world over.

Cuthbert Wiltshaw, a wealthy man, tall, distinguished looking with greying hair and thick horn-rimmed spectacles, lived an extremely comfortable life in his fourteen-roomed villa which he had named Estoril, standing in its own extensive grounds and surrounded on three sides by high hedges and beech trees, on Station Road, Barlaston. The house had good views across open farmland and the Trentham Park golf course, where Wiltshaw was a member. He lived with his wife, Alice Maud Mary Wiltshaw, who was the same age as himself, the daughter of the late Mr E. Tomkinson, Managing Clerk in a firm of Crewe solicitors. Alice had travelled widely, being interested in languages, and from time to time employed foreign students who came to this country to improve their English. They had four daughters, all of whom had been married at Barlaston parish church, which Cuthbert and his wife attended regularly. Mrs Wiltshaw lived a quiet life and did not go out much in the evenings, preferring to sit with her husband, reading or listening to the radio, but they were featured in the pages of the *Staffordshire Sentinel* from time to time when they attended the theatre or a charity performance.

They employed two servants, Florence Dorrell and Ada Barlow, who arrived each morning at around 8 a.m. and left around 5.15 p.m. in the afternoon. They also had a gardener and chauffeur, Roy Shenton, who had been with them only a short time, following the dismissal of his predecessor

The Golf Club at Trentham, where Cuthbert Wiltshaw would often call in on his way home from work. (Author's collection)

on 6 May 1952. The house had quite extensive grounds and Mr Wiltshaw rented out the kitchen garden, orchard and paddock to a Mr Challinor, who worked there with his assistant Mr Brooks.

Cuthbert Wiltshaw was a man of regular habits and normally returned home at around 6.30 p.m., when Alice would have his evening meal waiting for him. She was inclined to stoutness, but was always well dressed and usually wore one or two pieces from her extensive collection of expensive jewellery, which she kept in a jewellery case in the top drawer of the dressing table in their bedroom. On Wednesday 16 July 1952, Cuthbert Wiltshaw arrived home at about 6.20 p.m., entering by the back door, which he found open. This led into the scullery and thence into the kitchen, which he found to be in complete chaos. Thinking that there had been an accident of some kind, he went into the hall and discovered his wife's body lying on the floor near to the front door, her head and face a mass of wounds.

Quickly, he telephoned his near neighbour Dr H.J. Browne, who hurried round but on examination of the body could see immediately that there was no hope. Wiltshaw then rang for the police and within twenty minutes Superintendent Thomas Lockley, the chief of the Staffordshire CID, had arrived, with several of his men. Stoke-on-Trent city police also arrived within a short time; Mr Wiltshaw was an influential man in the area and the Chief Constable of Stoke,

Mr F.L. Bunn, was anxious that everything possible should be done to bring his wife's killer to justice. Close examination of the area showed that the attack had probably started in the kitchen and had then progressed to the hall, where Alice Wiltshaw had finally met her end. The attack had been a brutal one and there were cuts to the dead woman's hands that indicated that she had put up a spirited defence before succumbing to a hail of blows. In the kitchen, the floor appeared to have been recently cleaned and the table, which had bloodstains on it, was laid for a meal. Pieces of broken pottery lay alongside Mrs Wiltshaw's tortoiseshell spectacles and a saucepan handle and vegetables prepared for cooking were scattered about the floor. There were further bloodstains in the passage leading from the kitchen into the hall, and on the jamb of the communicating door were marks in blood that appeared to have been made by a gloved hand. In the hall were a hammer, an antique steel poker about 3ft long with a barb in the end and a piece of wood. The poker was bent, although the distraught Wiltshaw was certain that it had not been bent when he went out that morning. A quantity of water had been spilled in the kitchen and there were several footprints, which the police carefully protected and in the drawing room, that day's *Evening Sentinel* lay open on a small table and a lady's handbag lay discarded on the floor. It contained a chequebook, some personal papers and keys.

Within the hour, extensive roadblocks had been set up in Gaol Square, Stafford and at Newcastle-under-Lyme, where all north and southbound traffic was stopped. Drivers and their passengers were questioned and mobile police made random stops throughout the county. Later that evening and on the following morning, mental institutions, approved schools and Borstal institutions were checked for absconders.

Superintendent Lockley was soon able to announce that the police were anxious to interview a youth of between sixteen and twenty years who had been seen near the house earlier in the afternoon. He was reported to have been of average height and wearing grey clothing and this news immediately raised hopes of an early arrest, although in the end it came to nothing. Meanwhile, the body of Alice Wiltshaw was taken to the police mortuary to await a post-mortem by Professor J.M. Webster.

Lockley now had a dilemma on his hands – whether or not to call in Scotland Yard. The social standing of the dead woman's husband probably influenced him when he elected to do so and Superintendent Reg Spooner was summoned from London to assist, together with Detective Sergeant Millen. In the meantime, the local police had discovered that Mrs Wiltshaw had received a telephone call at 5.15 p.m. on the day of the murder, so the timescale for her killing had now been narrowed down considerably.

Out in the grounds, a police dog named Rex was assisting in the hunt for clues and eventually turned up a pair of hogskin gloves that had been thrown into some bushes at the rear of the house; size 8½ and made by Dents. The gloves were rather grubby and on the left-hand thumb was a tear, about half an inch long, which looked as though it had only been done very recently. One glove had a pearl button attached at the wrist; the one on the other glove was missing and was later found adjacent to Mrs Wiltshaw's body.

The following day, James Webster conducted a post-mortem on Alice Wiltshaw. He noted that she was a stout, elderly woman, 5ft 5½in in height. In life, she had suffered from a stiff right elbow joint which would have rendered that limb ineffective either in defence or offence. She had many grave injuries, from which a great deal of blood had been lost, including several stab wounds to the abdomen and right shoulder. The lower jaw was completely shattered and a large gaping wound extended from left of the bridge of the nose to the right ear. There were defensive wounds to the dead woman's ring finger that in the opinion of the doctor was definitely from the warding off of blows. The top of the skull had been beaten in and Webster thought that some of the wounds could have been caused by the steel poker found in the hall. Mrs Wiltshaw's blood was Group A but there were other stains belonging to Group O, notably on a raincoat. At the subsequent trial, Webster was to tell the court, 'In all my experience, I have never come across a case where such brutal and vicious blows have been struck by a murderer.'

Later that day, Cedric Wiltshaw handed to the police a list of items that he believed had been stolen by his wife's attacker. Altogether they numbered twenty-one items, Wiltshaw estimated the total value at £3,000. They included a lady's platinum and diamond wristlet watch, valued at £100, a diamond ruby and emerald swivel ring (£36), a sapphire and diamond ring (£50), a diamond baguette ring (£300), a platinum and diamond eternity ring (£30), an emerald and diamond bracelet (£230), a man's gold cigarette case, about £20 in notes and a man's RAF raincoat.

The police now turned their attention to possible suspects, including former employees of the Wiltshaws. One of these was a man named Leslie Green, aged 29, who had worked at Estoril as chauffeur and gardener from 22 October 1950 until 6 May 1952 and the police were interested to hear that Mr Wiltshaw had dismissed the man on that date for taking time off without permission and for using Wiltshaw's Rover motorcar for his own use. Apart from his normal duties, Green regularly entered the house to clean out the fire grates and to fill the bin with logs. He would also clean the windows upstairs and down and so was familiar with the whole of the house. Mr Wiltshaw would perhaps not have been keen to employ his chauffeur in the first place, had he known that the man had a criminal record and had received various periods of imprisonment for theft, including three years in Borstal in November 1943 and a month for being in possession of two firearms without a license. However, a report from the Borstal institution stated that there was 'A reasonable probability that Green will abstain from crime and lead a useful and industrious life' and he was recommended for discharge on 28 February 1945. The report noted that Green was a serving soldier and would be returned direct to the army.

Leslie Green's army mug shot. (National Archives)

Green himself was nowhere to be found, but the police soon located his address at 16 Elmore Avenue, Blurton, Stoke-on-Trent, where his wife Constance was living with her 6-year-old daughter, Gillian. She was able to tell the police that her husband had been in the army from 1939 to 1949, however this was not strictly correct, for Green had been in prison for three of those years and had thereafter worked as a van driver. Constance did not seem surprised that the police were looking for her husband, although at the time she had not been told why. 'He was in the habit of going off without notice', she told them, and she suspected that he had a girlfriend somewhere.

Meanwhile, as the police continued their search for the missing man, the newspapers were posting banner headlines about the shocking murder: 'ACE SCOTLAND YARD MAN CALLED TO BARLASTON MURDER' screamed the *Staffordshire Sentinel*, 'NIGHT POLICE SEARCH FOLLOWS BRUTAL BARLASTON MURDER' said the *Advertiser*, eager not to be beaten by its rival. Soon the papers included the fact that a man, Leslie Green, was wanted for questioning and on 23 July a stocky young man, 5ft 5in in height, with a boyish face and a shock of dark hair walked into Longton police station and announced to the astonished WPC Edna Maud Bowers, 'I am the man you are all shouting after!' He was dressed in a light sports jacket and worsted trousers and was carrying a small valise, in which were items of clothing and a pair of crêpe-soled shoes.

Superintendent Spooner, together with Detective Chief Superintendent Lockley and Detective Sergeant Millen lost no time in confronting Green and in reply to Spooner's question, 'Why have you come here?' Green replied, 'I saw in the papers that you wanted to see me'. Spooner said to him, 'We propose to question you as to your knowledge of the matter at Barlaston and your movements on the day in question'. Green appeared unmoved and merely replied, 'Alright.'

Sergeant Millen took down a statement in longhand, part of which read as follows:

On Thursday July 17 1952, I left the Metropole Hotel in Leeds, at about 10.30 a.m. to go home for the weekend. I bought a paper and returned to the hotel at 11.30 a.m. I had the *Daily Express* and read of the murder of Mrs Wiltshaw at Barlaston. As I was staying at the Metropole in the name of Wiltshaw of Estoril, I went back to the hotel and told the receptionist it was a relative and I would have to go immediately. As I came out of the hotel, I met two chaps I knew, one called Lorenzo and the other Charles. I had first met Lorenzo at the Cameo Ballroom in Longton when I worked there in the evenings. They were supposed to meet me in Spinks's bar in Briggate near the station on the previous Monday evening. I had told them about a fortnight previously to get me two rings, an engagement ring and a wedding ring, as I wanted to give them to Nora (my girlfriend). I went to keep my appointment but they didn't come in. When I saw them on the 17th, I asked them if they had got my rings and Lorenzo said, 'Yes.' He gave the two rings in little ring cases and I asked them if they had any money. Between them, they gave me £15 [a curious transaction, seeing that Lorenzo and Charles had just handed over two rings, for which they had received no money from Green]. Altogether, I had about £50 from them over the past eight weeks. They did not give me the money for any special reason. I had a drink and then went to meet Nora at her address. I gave her the rings and she said they were very nice and that was all. Next day, she said she had heard from her sister that the police were looking for me. I said I didn't know what they wanted and she gave me the rings back. Nora left me just after this and I had a walk round, thinking what I was going to say about the police wanting me and while I was doing that, I threw the rings away in the canal from the bridge just opposite the Golden Lion. I have not seen Lorenzo or Charles since July the 17th. When I first met Lorenzo eight weeks ago, he asked me where I was working and I told him. He asked me if the house was worth breaking into and I said 'No,' as I was working there at the time or had just finished. It was either then or later that he asked me if there was any jewellery there and I said, 'I suppose so.' It was either then or later that he asked me how to get into the house. I just said that there were two doors, one at the front and one at the back. At no time did I agree with him to break into the house and I can't say who killed Mrs Wiltshaw. It did pass through my mind that it might have been Lorenzo and Charles but that is all. I have never discussed with anybody how to get into the house or about the fields at the back, nor about the lane that is cut through from Broughton Crescent to the fields.

The valise was then produced and C.S. Lockley said, 'I understand that this property belongs to you?' Green answered, 'Yes, that's right.' Green was then taken to Stone police station where he told Lockley that he didn't do the murder, but knew that he was involved and perhaps was responsible for the events in some way.

On 23 July, at Longton police station, a much longer statement was made by Green, in which he described having seen an advertisement in the *Sentinel* for a chauffeur/handyman at the Wiltshaws' house. He was paid £7 a week and had a uniform provided. He worked for Mr Wiltshaw until May 1952 when he was given a week's notice for using the car without permission. He used to go to work in old army clothes and change in the garage. After he left Estoril, he got a job as a bricklayer's labourer. He and his wife were buying their own house through a building society and to help with the money his wife worked as well. He then started to work as a van driver for Garners, seedsmen at Newcastle. He stayed with them until three weeks ago, when he left. Some time in May 1952, he met a girl called Nora Lammey at the Astoria Dance Hall in Leeds. She was the same age as him and told him that she was a nurse. He introduced himself as 'Terry' and from then on he met the girl regularly, telling her that he was single. When he left Garners, he returned home to his family and travelled back to Leeds at weekends. He then flew to Belfast where Nora Lammey's parents lived and spent two or three days with her there. When he flew back, he booked in at the Metropole Hotel, Leeds, under the name of L. Wiltshaw, of Estoril, Barlaston. On Saturday, he saw Nora in the afternoon and at 2.40 a.m. the following morning he caught the train to London, where he booked into the Strand Hotel under the name of Colin Jones. The journey to London appears to have been somewhat pointless for he was soon back on the train, this time to Stafford on 16 July, from where he said that he hoped to go home to patch things up with his wife.

At the Station Hotel, Stafford, he chatted to one or two people and at 3.30 p.m. went into the dining room. He stayed in the hotel drinking and then left at about 5 p.m., going into a nearby park where he sat down and dozed off. He then went back to the Station Hotel, where he had left his bag, before catching a train to Leeds, where he went back to the Metropole Hotel. (At no time did Green mention where he got the money for all this travelling.) He stayed at the hotel until Sunday evening, spending most of his time with Nora Lammey. Telling Nora that he had to go to Torquay on business, he left his girlfriend at 3 a.m. on the Monday and made two more aimless journeys, first to Newton Abbott and then to Shrewsbury, from where he telephoned Nora and arranged to meet her in Birmingham, as she was travelling down on her way to Stourbridge. They parted at 7.30 p.m., after which he caught a train to Stafford and arrived at his home at about 2 a.m. Unable to wake anyone in the house, he spent the night in the outside toilet until 8 a.m., when his wife, who had been staying next door, came home. The final words of the statement were, 'I was not in Barlaston or in fact near Barlaston or Stafford on Wednesday afternoon, July 16.' This statement took over four hours to complete.

On 24 July, Green, having had the night to think things over, gave a third, more detailed statement to the police:

I am clear in my mind what I did on Wednesday 16 July 1952. I know I arrived at Stafford railway station round about 10 a.m. on the Wednesday morning and round about 1.30 p.m. went to the Station Hotel. I went into the hotel bar and noticed two men talking to the barman [actually the hotel manager]. Two other men came up and I remained with the four of them until 3.30 p.m., then we ordered lunch and went into the dining room. We finished around 4.30 p.m. and then went into the upstairs lounge. We stayed for quarter of an hour and then I began to feel dizzy from the drink I had taken, including a bottle of wine between us at lunch. I made the excuse I was going to catch a train and left the hotel at 5 p.m., going across the road to the park, where I must have dozed off as it was about quarter to six when I got back to the hotel. Before I went to the hotel, I got my bag from the station cloakroom. I walked back into the hotel and the manager asked me if I had fallen asleep and missed my train – I answered 'Yes.'

I then had a wash and brush up and went to have some dinner. The same waitress served me as at lunchtime. I left the hotel at 6.30 p.m. to 6.45 p.m. and booked a ticket to Leeds 3rd class. The train was due to go after 7 p.m. and I had a long conversation with the ticket collector, which lasted ten to fifteen minutes. I got on the train and had to change at Stretford and I arrived at Leeds after midnight and went to the Metropole. Leaving my bag there, I went to the Nursing Home but didn't see Nora – I saw the Night Sister.

If this statement could be verified in all respects, then Green would have an alibi for the time of the murder, but there was still the vital period between 5 p.m. and 5.45 p.m. for which he claimed to have dozed off on the park bench.

The police by now had contacted Nora Lammey, who told them that she had met Green in the last week of April. After that, she met him fairly regularly and it is clear that she was smitten with the chauffeur, who used his employer's car to take her to a medical dinner on 2 May. Between 23 June and 9 July, she travelled to her parents' home in Ireland, where Green visited her on two occasions, travelling by air. When in Ireland, Green proposed and she accepted, being promised an engagement ring as soon as Green could

Stafford station and the Station Hotel. (Staffordshire Arts & Museum Service)

arrange it. They then visited a local Presbyterian clergyman and obtained a marriage license so that they could get married as soon as possible. The couple agreed that Nora would give up her job at the nursing home on 21 July and that they would marry shortly after. According to the girl, Green had told her that he worked as a representative for a pottery firm and had travelled extensively in America. On 17 July, having returned to Leeds, Nora met Green at the Metropole Hotel and her erstwhile fiancé gave her two rings; a five-stone diamond baguette and an eternity ring, one of which was a little too big. No doubt Nora was on a high at this point, for she was going to get married to her good-looking sweetheart and she was now the possessor of expensive jewellery, but her euphoria did not last long. The following day, 18 July, she received a letter from her sister in Belfast telling her that the local police had been enquiring after a man named Leslie Green, but she had not at first connected him with the man her sister knew as 'Terry.' For the first time, Nora began to feel the first pangs of doubt about her beloved and asked him for an explanation. Green, unperturbed, promised that he would make enquiries and find out why the police were looking for him. This explanation does not seem to have settled Nora's worries, for she handed the rings back to him, although they still continued to meet and went to the cinema the next evening, where they saw *It Won't Be a Stylish Marriage*, a title that Nora might have found a little unsettling.

Whatever doubts Nora Lammey might have been entertaining, she was still very much in love with Green and she introduced him to a colleague at the nursing home, Greta Davies, who agreed to allow Green to use her flat at 16B, Belmont Gardens, Leeds, that weekend, while she was away with her husband.

She claimed to have had no idea that her colleague Nora was to share the flat as well and according to Nora, she occupied one bedroom and Green the other, a statement that was received with some incredulity by the police. While he was talking to Greta Davies, Green produced the two rings and told her that his aunt, Mrs Wiltshaw, had been murdered with an old-fashioned poker. He claimed that his uncle had told him to 'get on his way,' as the police were 'roping everybody in.' Green had also shown the rings to another nurse, Beatrice Turner, at 1 a.m. on 17 July, only seven hours after the murder.

On 30 July, Green was examined by Professor Webster, who found three significant injuries. An area of scrape abrasions on the front of the right wrist, now scabbed over and consistent, so Webster thought, with it having been caused on or about 16 July, a similar type of wound close to the ball of the right thumb and a small wound on the left thumb which matched the small cut in the left-hand glove which had been found at Estoril.

The headline in Sunday's *News of the World* screamed 'MOST VICIOUS MURDER OF THE CENTURY' and detailed a trail of broken vases, overturned furniture and blood-spattered carpets. Matters now proceeded quickly, as more witnesses came forward and were interviewed. Nurse Davies' flat was searched from top to bottom and in a small, brick-lined coal house, hidden away in a cavity formed by an incomplete brick, 8ft from the floor, were the two rings that Mrs Davies and Nurse Turner both identified as being the ones Green had shown to them.

C.S. Lockley formally charged Green with the murder of Alice Wiltshaw on 6 August, and then conducted two identification parades, when three local women tried to identify a man that they had seen in Broughton Crescent (the road which ran up the side of Estoril) on the afternoon of the murder. The parades were rather inconclusive, only Mrs Nora Hind, a near neighbour of the Wiltshaws, picking out Green as the man she had seen. Unfortunately, she also pointed to another man at the same time, saying, 'It is one of those.'

The police had by then discovered that on the day of the murder, the 5.10 p.m. train from Stafford arrived at Barlaston at 5.35 p.m. and Estoril was only 200 yards from the station. There was a train back at 6.05 p.m. which arrived at Stafford at 6.26 p.m., almost the exact times Green was supposed to have been asleep in the park, and the police were now certain that they had enough evidence to proceed to trial. Committal proceedings were held on 26 November and the trial itself began on 1 December 1952 in front of Mr Justice Stable, a lawyer who was known not to mince his words. The hearing had attracted much attention locally and almost two hours before the hearing was due to start, over fifty people were queuing for admission. For the Crown appeared Mr E. Ryder Richardson QC with Mr J.F. Bourke and for the defence, Mr G.G. Baker QC and Mr G.T. Meredith. The accused man, dressed in a green suit with a spotted tie, entered the dock and in a clear, firm voice pleaded 'Not Guilty.'

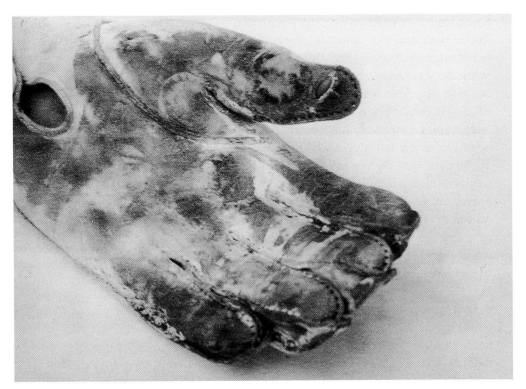

The left-hand glove found at Estoril. Note the small tear on the thumb. (National Archives)

The prosecution began by telling the jury that over forty witnesses would be produced and that the weight of circumstantial evidence was so great that there could be no reasonable doubt as to the guilt of the accused man. Cedric Wiltshaw, obviously deeply affected by having to go over the details of his wife's death again, said that his wife was very fond of jewellery, but had no enemies and no one to fear. She was guarded only by a small dog and was in the habit of leaving the kitchen door unlocked.

The manager of the Station Hotel, Stafford, Geoffrey Lionel Farr, gave his story regarding the times he saw Green on the day of the murder and about an RAF-type raincoat that Green had been carrying. Defence counsel produced another coat and questioned him closely about it, but Farr was adamant that the coat he had seen Green carrying was nothing like it. He told the court that he had gone off duty at about 3.30 p.m., coming back at 6 p.m. and that he did not see Green between those hours.

Then the prosecution turned to the impressions of feet on the kitchen floor at Estoril. The floor had been taken up and was now exhibited in an adjoining room, so that both judge and jury could inspect it. Photographs of the footprints were exhibited alongside the crêpe-soled shoes taken from the accused. A member of the fingerprint branch at New Scotland Yard,

Chief Inspector Holten, told the court that 'These shoes could have made the impressions on the portions of the tiles of the kitchen floor.' Defence counsel made much of the fact that Holten's actual job was with fingerprints and that normally sixteen points of similarity were required when bringing fingerprint evidence to court. He now tried to extend this practice to the photographs of the ridges on the crêpe-soled shoes before the court. Photographs A and B had around twelve ridges clearly visible, but photograph C had more than seventeen. Chief Inspector Holten insisted that the marks on the tiles could have been made by Green's shoes but had to agree that many other shoes of the same manufacture could also have made them.

Nora Lammey caused great interest when she went into the witness box and said that she had met Green in April and on 2 May he had taken her to a dance in a Rover motorcar. He had visited her twice in Ireland and on the second occasion had proposed marriage and she had accepted him. She thought that her fiancé was quite wealthy. After having obtained the necessary marriage license in Belfast, they had tentatively fixed the marriage date for 9 August.

She said that Green had told her that he had lost his raincoat, which had been stolen from the cloakroom of the Metropole Hotel in Leeds. He also told her that his wallet had been stolen. Later, he told her that these items had been returned to him by the police. The court then adjourned for lunch and the judge arranged for Miss Lammey to have hers in a private room and asked her not to discuss the case with anyone during the break.

On resuming, Nurse Lammey said that she saw Green on the evening of 17 July, when he gave her the two rings. At this stage she was asked to try on the rings, produced as evidence, which she did, remarking that one was 'a bit tight'. In fact, when she tried to remove the ring, she could not and the judge ordered a brief recess while she went into an adjoining room with a policewoman, returning successfully after a few minutes. On that night, she told the court, she had noticed a bandage on Green's wrist and later that evening, when they were at the nursing home, she noticed another bandage on his arm. She was aware that the police were looking for a man with scratches on him and when she mentioned it, Green had replied dismissively, 'They would find lots of scratches on me.' The judge asked, 'At that time, on 17 July, had you read about the death of Mrs Wiltshaw in the papers?' 'Only a short account,' was her reply. 'Up to that time, had it crossed your mind in any shape or form he could possibly be connected with it?' 'No,' she answered.

On Friday 18 July, Norah saw Green at 3 p.m. outside the nursing home and Green had shown her some ring cases, which he said were for her rings, but she had given the rings back to him. At this stage, the judge lost patience and snapped, 'Miss Lammey, try and get some realism into your story.' The girl then explained that she had given the rings back after receiving the letter from her sister in Ireland.

She also said that on the Sunday night, when they went to the station for the 10.20 p.m. train, Green had told her for the first time that he was not who she thought he was and that he was out of work. This prompted another outburst from Mr Justice Stable, who was beginning to prove a little unstable at this point. He was incredulous that Miss Lammey should have shown little or no reaction to this surprising news, seeing that she had just given up her job. Further questioning produced the reply that Green had told her that he had been employed by the Wiltshaw family as a chauffeur. He had also said that although he had nothing to do with the murder, he knew who had done it and mentioned the name 'Charles.' She also said that Green told her that he had been in Stafford on the day of the crime and that he had spent the afternoon drinking. She had shown him a newspaper on 22 July because his name was mentioned and he replied that if he had done it (the robbery), it would have been done in a different way. The judge interjected, 'In other words he was saying that if he had done the robbery, it would not have involved murder.' Nurse Lammey agreed.

The footprint found in the kitchen at Estoril. (National Archives)

After two and a half hours, Nurse Lammey's ordeal ended and she left the witness box looking exhausted and upset. She was followed by Sister Beatrice Turner who told the court she had been shown the rings by the accused, who had also offered her a cigarette from a gold case, but when she asked to look at it, he had closed it and quickly put it in his pocket. Green had told her that he was going to marry Nurse Lammey and hinted that he was going to buy a bungalow for them to live in, costing £4,500.

Alfred Blackburn, who had been a patient at the nursing home, told the court that Green had asked him for money on two occasions and on one occasion, he took out a wallet and showed him the contents, which included several new £1 notes and a chequebook. Jack Higgins, a gardener employed by Leeds Corporation, was called to say that he had found two ring boxes in an iris bed in Park Square Gardens on 30 July.

Chief Superintendent Lockley was next to give evidence and the gloves found in the garden at Estoril were produced. Lockley said that he had asked the accused to try the gloves on and noticed that the small hole on the pad of the thumb of the left-hand glove matched exactly with a small abrasion on Green's thumb. Lockley was also asked about the footprints in the kitchen and in particular about the number of people who had 'paddled' about the floor. 'Six police officers, six civilians and himself,' was the reply.

On Wednesday 3 December, the case proceeded and Nurse Davies gave her evidence, followed by Gwynneth Dorothy Jenkins, a receptionist at the Metropole Hotel. She said that a 'Terry Wiltshaw' had sent a letter from the Strand Hotel in London, booking a room at the Metropole for the night of 17 July. She could not remember whether or not he had said that his raincoat and wallet had been stolen or lost. Kenneth Bleasby, a porter at the hotel, said that Green had offered him a cigarette from a 'gold looking' cigarette case.

Professor Webster then gave his evidence and the judge told him that it would not be necessary for him to go into minute detail of the wounds to Mrs Wiltshaw's body. He had also withheld several photographs from the jury as being too distressing for them to see. (When this file was seen by the author under the Freedom of Information Act, having been embargoed since 1952, the photographs were absent.)

On Thursday 4 December, it was the turn of the accused man to enter the witness box. His examination-in-chief lasted nearly two and a half hours and he began by denying that he had killed Alice Wiltshaw, or that he had stolen rings or any other jewellery from her. Mr Baker then announced that Green would be the only witness for the defence. He opened by asking;

Mr Baker: 'First of all you made a long statement to the police in which you dealt in considerable detail with your visit to Ireland with Nora Lammey and how you met her?'
Green: 'Yes.'
Mr Baker: 'Is that account substantially accurate?'
Green 'Substantially.'

Then followed detailed questioning about the state of Green's finances, during which he admitted that while staying at the Strand Palace Hotel, he had stolen a wallet from a handbag, which had been left unattended. This had produced about £15.

The RAF raincoat that Mr Wiltshaw had recognised as his own was then produced. It had been found on a train at Holyhead and Green denied stoutly that he had ever seen it before. He also denied again that he had been anywhere near Estoril on 16 July or that he had the mackintosh in his possession. The marks on his arm, which he showed to the judge and jury, had been caused when he was walking on Ilkley Moor about ten days before the murder.

He was then closely questioned by counsel for the Crown and repeated that a man named Lorenzo had given him two rings, a gold cigarette case and other items in Leeds on 17 July. He hid the rings in Davies's flat in Leeds and had sold the other pieces. He admitted that he had sent Superintendent Spooner on a wild goose chase by telling him that he had thrown the rings and the cases into the river. Mr Ryder Richardson pointed out to him that before 16 July, he was short of money and that after that date he had plenty. Green replied that he had got the money by stealing. Further questioning elicited the reply that Green knew that Mrs Wiltshaw would be alone in the house between 5.30 p.m. and 6.30 p.m., but that he had not gone to the house on the 16th, neither did he kill her. He also denied that the mark on his thumb matched the hole in the glove, insisting that the evidence regarding that injury was rigged by the police. Mr Baker then asked about Lorenzo and Charles, and why these men had given him so much money. Green mumbled a reply to the effect that Lorenzo was hoping that Green would help him in some criminal enterprise.

Towards the end of his interrogation, Mr Ryder Richardson asked Green whether he was rather an accomplished liar? Again the judge interrupted, suggesting that the word 'accomplished' should be replaced by 'consistent.' Green could do nothing but agree. He also said that he had obtained money prior to 16 July by involvement in various criminal activities and that he always had a fair amount of money in his pocket. Once again, Mr Justice Stable interrupted with a bluntness that was by now beginning to seem familiar to the court.

Justice Stable: 'Green, let us get down to brass tacks about this. You told us that it was untrue that you had your wallet stolen or lost with £40 in it. You are saying that by Sunday morning, the 13th, however much money you had, it had all been stolen?'

Green: 'No Sir.'

Justice Stable: 'Had none been stolen?'

Green: 'No Sir'.

Justice Stable: 'You were prepared to borrow money from Nurse Lammey and others while you had enough money to pay your hotel bill?'

Green: 'Yes, because I needed the money.'

Finally, counsel for the prosecution referred to the 'old-fashioned poker' with which the prosecution alleged the murder had been committed. 'Did you tell Nurse Davies that Mrs Wiltshaw had been killed by an old-fashioned poker?' Ryder Richardson asked. 'I don't remember that.' 'Nurse Davies said that you did', shot back Ryder Richardson. 'How did you know Mrs Wiltshaw had been killed with a poker like that?' 'If I did say that, I must have read about it in a paper,' was the reply.

Greta Davies's flat. The far door on the right leads to the coal place, where Leslie Green hid the rings. (National Archives)

Which paper?' Ryder Richardson snapped. 'I suggest you cannot find any newspaper in which the description of an old-fashioned poker is given prior to July 19 or 20?'

Yet again, the judge leaned over to make a point. 'Think carefully over the question – take all the time you want.' When Green could only repeat that he had 'read of the poker in the newspapers,' copies of several morning papers for 17 and 18 July were brought into court and scanned closely by the judge and the accused. Finally, it was clear that no mention had been made of the fact that Mrs Wiltshaw was killed by a poker, although one newspaper did say that the dead woman had used a poker to defend herself. Nowhere was the phrase 'old-fashioned' used.

The afternoon was now drawing on and the judge intimated that he would start his summing up on the next morning after final speeches from counsel. Mr Ryder Richardson made it quite clear to the jury that the case for the prosecution had been proved beyond any question of doubt and Mr Baker completed his final submissions for the defence on the morning of 5 December by admitting that 'The murder was possibly unparalleled in its bestiality,' a reminder that was probably the worst thing that he could have said to the jury.

He pointed out that none of the other jewellery missing from Estoril had turned up or had been traced to the prisoner. He also complained that the prosecution had not called the four men who had been in the Station Hotel with Green. He had to admit that Green himself had said that the evidence pointed to him and it would be foolish to try to gainsay the matter. He reminded the jury that three women had inspected an identity parade of eleven men and two had failed. The other had only picked out Green at the second attempt and while it could not be denied that Green knew the Wiltshaws and was familiar with Estoril, this surely pointed away from him as the perpetrator of the crime. 'If he has any sense at all,' Baker told the jury, 'and if he has anything, he has sense, he was going to be very chary about going back to a place from where he had been dismissed.'

Dealing with the marks on the kitchen floor, Baker complained that the evidence of the Scotland Yard officer had not differentiated between sole and heel. All he could say was that the spaces between the ridges were about the same. There were many people milling about in the kitchen that afternoon and no evidence of elimination had been presented to the court. The marks could have been left by anybody wearing similar shoes. A telling point was that no trace of pottery fragments or bloodstains had been found on the shoes and when Green returned to the Station Hotel, he was in no way distressed or ruffled, as one might expect from a man who had just committed an horrific murder.

His final sentence was in the form of a question to the accused man, 'Did you have any part in the killing?' 'No,' was the reply.

At 11.45 a.m. on 5 December, the judge started his summing up by telling the jury that Green was a liar and a thief, but noted that where there was a conflict of evidence, they should accept the construction most favourable to the prisoner. The burden of proof lay on the prosecution and the jury could not bring in a verdict of guilty unless they were fully satisfied, after reviewing the whole of the evidence. If on the other hand, the jury were satisfied that the accused was guilty, they would do their duty. In this case, he told the jury, the prosecution alleged that Green had not gone to Estoril to kill, but to steal. The prosecution maintained that Green had been surprised by Mrs Wiltshaw, who recognised him immediately and that had precipitated the savage attack upon her. Timing was also of the essence, the judge said, and if the jury accepted those put forward by the prosecution, Green would have had two and a half hours to get from Stafford to Barlaston, commit the crime and return to Stafford. During all that time no one appeared to have seen him, nor was there anyone who could substantiate Green's own story of the snooze in the park.

The summing up lasted three and a half hours and the jury were then sent out to make their decision. They were absent for less than half an hour and returned with a verdict of guilty, whereupon Green was sentenced to hang. Turning smartly, flanked by two warders, he was taken down to the cells.

In the eighteen days between sentence and execution, Green occupied himself by reading *A Son of the People* by Baroness Orczy, a life of Hopalong Cassidy and H.V. Morton's *Through the Lands of the Bible*. While in gaol, he suffered from a bad cold and, it seems, had only one handkerchief. He also had toothache and had the tooth extracted by the prison dentist. He remained in touch with Nora Lammey and wrote asking her to send him some postage stamps, as he was only allowed one official stamp per week. His hopes for a reprieve were dashed by a letter dated 20 December 1952 from the Home Secretary, stating that there was no reason to interfere with the due process of the law.

Estoril, where Alice Maud Wiltshaw was beaten to death. (Now part of the Wedgwood Memorial Museum.) (Author's collection)

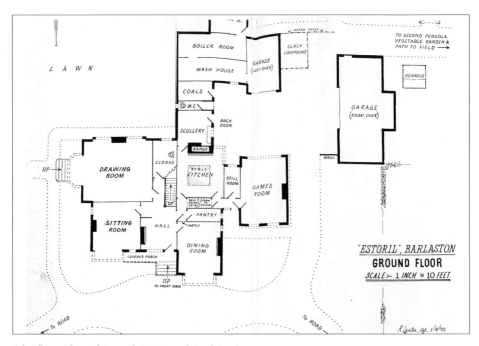

The floor plan of Estoril. (National Archives)

Barlaston halt, less than 200 yards from Estoril. (Author's collection)

An undated and anonymous letter was sent to Green from Spring House, Biddulph Moor, Stoke-on-Trent. It read:

Dear Leslie,
I have certain reasons to believe that it was not by your own will that you murdered Mrs Wiltshaw and because of this, I ask you one question. I have all the needed evidence to stop you hanging except one thing. Did your girl friend really make you love her or was her love ingenuine? [*sic*]. If you answer 'Yes,' I have enough facts to check this answer. If you answer 'No,' I have more.

The letter was signed 'Ten of Clubs' and turned out to have been written by a 10-year-old boy, living in Spring House, who had no grounds whatsoever for his assertions!

As usual, an examination into Green's mental state was carried out by the Principal Medical Officer of Holloway Prison, Dr Thomas Christie, who reported, 'He is an intelligent man of the soldierly type, smart, alert, quick to understand and reply to questions and capable of sustaining conversation in a relevant manner. His general bearing is that of a trained soldier and there is nothing in his appearance or conduct to suggest mental abnormality.'

On 23 December 1952, the day of the execution, only a handful of people stood outside Winson Green Prison at 9 a.m., while a few yards away Albert Pierrepoint and Syd Dernley were carrying out the sentence of the law and Leslie Green fell 6ft 8in to his death. At no stage had Green shown any signs of remorse and he took to his grave the whereabouts of the missing £2,750 worth of jewellery.

Shortly afterwards, a letter was received by the prison governor from Green's widow, Constance, asking for her husband's property to be sent to her. Green had requested that all his property should be sent to Nora Lammey, now living in Golders Green, but he had failed to put this request in writing and the governor was instructed to release what little Green had left, including a Rolls Razor, a Ronson lighter and two wristwatches, to his wife.

Cuthbert Wiltshaw, unable to stand the atmosphere in the house where his beloved Alice Maud had been so cruelly killed, sold it almost immediately and it is now part of the Wedgwood Memorial College. Less than two minutes walk away, the tiny railway station of Barlaston still stands, lonely and so convenient on that day in 1952, when Leslie Green extracted a terrible revenge for his dismissal. A few yards further down the road, the Plume of Feathers public house, now somewhat altered and enlarged, stands by the Trent & Mersey Canal, where the unfortunate Christina Collins feared for her life 113 years earlier.

11

SUICIDE BY JUDICIAL HANGING

Wilslock, 1955

The *Evening Sentinel* for Saturday 26 February 1955 bore a banner headline, 'STABBED MAN IN CAR DIES: STAFFS. MURDER HUNT ON.' There followed fifteen column inches detailing the discovery of a man, Donald Haywood Lainton, aged 28, of 234 Dialstone Lane, Stockport, an insurance broker's agent, in his car on the lane leading to Birchen Bower Farm, Willslock, near Uttoxeter on the previous day. Lainton was then still alive, but appeared to have suffered a frenzied attack with a sharp implement and the inside of the car, a Ford Prefect, number 7785H, was heavily bloodstained. It had been snowing and the car was embedded in a snowdrift several feet deep when it was spotted by Mr Bernard Bettson, a retired farmer, who was visiting his wife's father, Mr Arthur Derry, at the farm. Mr Bettson was in the act of chopping wood when he saw the car in the lane at about 1.45 p.m. The car appeared to be stuck and as he watched, a man got out and rocked the front bumper. Bettson was evidently neither bothered about the driver's predicament, nor of a mind to go and see if he could help, for he turned and went into the house for his lunch. However, at 3 p.m., his wife Elizabeth noticed that the car was still there and curious, despite the inclement weather, she put on a coat and walked down the rough track towards the vehicle, noticing that the front wheels were in a little rut off the lane and the back wheels on it. Peering inside the vehicle, she saw that the back of the driver's seat was pushed forward against the steering wheel and a brief case was propped up on the back seat. Between the seats, on the floor of the car, she could just make out what appeared to be a man's knees sticking up. While she was still trying to work out what had happened, a milk wagon drove up and stopped. The driver, John Johnson, and his mate came over and Johnson drew attention to a pool of blood under the driver's seat. An overcoat was lying on the floor that appeared to have been placed there to conceal a man's body, for under it he could see a trousered knee and a man's wrist sticking out. A cup and a bottle of milk lay on the floor behind the driver's seat and a mackintosh lay over the back of the seat, while on the rear seat lay a trilby hat.

Dialstone Lane, Stockport, where Donald Lainton lived. (Author's collection)

Despite the fact that it was obvious to them all that the car contained an injured man, neither of the three made any attempt to explore the interior of the vehicle further and, leaving the other two, Johnson got back into his lorry and drove to the nearby Red Lion pub, where he telephoned for an ambulance. On his way to the Red Lion, he met Dr Charles James Coventry, of Howitt Place, Uttoxeter who followed him back to the farm in his own motorcar and, after speaking to Mr Bettson, went to the abandoned vehicle and opened the offside rear door. He saw the body of a man, unconscious but still breathing, with a small wound over the right eyebrow. The right eye itself was almost unrecognisable, such was its condition and the tissue around it was enormously swollen and discoloured. There was also another small wound on the left side of the neck, while the man's hair and face were soaked with blood, and there was a trickle coming from his mouth.

Just then, the ambulance arrived and with care, the man was lifted out of the car and taken to Stafford General Infirmary, where Surgical Registrar Balwant Singh Khehar admitted him to casualty. The injured man had been well wrapped up against the cold and was wearing an overcoat, a leather jerkin, a blue suit, woollen scarf, black shoes and one brown leather glove, the other being found down the farm lane by the police a while later. He was bleeding freely from the nose and was deeply unconscious. On examination, Dr Khehar found puncture wounds in the head, over the chest, on the left side of the neck and on the right hand. The pulse was irregular and it was clear that the injured man's condition was serious and was deteriorating.

Hurriedly, he was taken down to X-ray, which showed a right side traumatic pneumothorax (air trapped within the chest cavity, usually caused after blunt or penetrating trauma to the chest) together with a general shrinking of the lung. Meanwhile, back at the farm, PC Frederick Arthur Phillips had been called to the scene and found the snow round the abandoned car heavily trampled and bloodstained below the offside rear door.

The registration number of the car enabled the police to identify the man as Donald Lainton and his wife, Kathleen, was called and spent an anxious night at her husband's bedside. A police constable, who was there to catch any words that the injured man might say, especially if he could describe his attacker, stayed with her, but unfortunately Lainton died at 3.55 a.m. on the Saturday morning. This was now a murder case, the cause of death being given as shock, following multiple injuries to the chest and brain. The police made a quick decision to call in the Scotland Yard murder team and within a short time Detective Superintendent Stephen Glander and Detective Sergeant Bruce were on the train north to Stafford.

The immediate reaction of the police was that Lainton had been stabbed during a robbery (although Kathleen Lainton told them that he would not have been carrying much money) and that it may not have happened where the car was found abandoned. The lane to Birchen Bower Farm, running off the Uttoxeter road, was narrow and once a vehicle had gone more than a few yards down the track, it would have been invisible from the main road. The lane petered out when it reached the farm and was not overlooked by any other buildings – it was therefore a possibility that whoever had driven the car to that spot was a local man who knew the lane well. The driver had obviously made a hasty getaway from the scene of the crime and an appeal was immediately launched for any motorist who had picked up a pedestrian in that area on Friday 25 February.

Detective Superintendent Lockley visited the scene and a dozen policemen searched the area with spades and rakes, looking for anything that might have been the murder weapon, which it was thought was probably some kind of dagger. Ice on the lane leading to the farm was too hard packed for footprints, but impressions in the soft snow at the side of the drive were photographed. Meanwhile, Professor Webster performed a post-mortem on the murdered man.

Kathleen Lainton told the police that her husband, who had worked for Roberts & Sons, of Marple, for the past five years, had left his home on 25 February to do business in Sutton Coldfield. She thought that he was carrying about £5 in a brown leather wallet and he had taken with him his chequebook and a red flask of tea. She identified the flask in the car as belonging to her husband, because of a long crack in the casing, secured with sellotape.

Fingerprints on the wing of the car, probably made during an attempt to free it from the snowdrift, led the police to Frederick Arthur Cross, a 33-year-old

The lonely track leading to Birchen Bower Farm.
(Author's collection)

concrete moulder who lived in a converted Nissen hut on an abandoned airfield at Hillside, Farley, Great Haywood, a few miles away from the farm. Police visited the address but Cross was not there, although there was evidence of a large fire in the living room grate and a large amount of ash. Detective Inspector Tucker took possession of a blue duffle coat and a pair of boots that appeared to be bloodstained and a neighbour told him that Cross had probably gone to his mother-in-law's house at 2 Maudsley Cottages, Great Alne, Alcester and it was there that the police found him. His mother-in-law, Mrs Annie Hilda Batchelor, had been warned by telegram that he was coming to stay for a few days. Detective Inspector Sydney Bates, of the Warwickshire Constabulary, approached Cross and began to tell him, 'We are police officers...' but Cross interrupted, saying, 'I know what you want me for' and pointing to his mother-in-law, went on, 'Don't say anything more. Tell me outside. Don't upset this lady. When I get to the police station, I'll tell you.' According to Mrs Batchelor, her son-in-law had seemed normal when he arrived at her house and showed no signs of distress but she also told the police that her daughter, Hilda Cross, had complained to her on several occasions that her husband had knocked her about and had smashed articles of furniture. She was also aware that Hilda had left her husband for a time, earlier that year.

Cross was taken to Stratford-on-Avon police station, and there he freely admitted that he was responsible for the death of Donald Lainton. He told Detective Inspector Bates that he had not used a knife to kill Lainton, but one half of an old pair of scissors, which he had thrown away in a field near the abandoned car. When searched, a tin of Rodine rat poison had been found in his pocket and he confessed that he had had thoughts of suicide but had been unable to go through with it. In reply to questioning, he insisted that robbery was not his motive for the killing.

He was collected by Superintendent Glander and Detective Constable Richard Eardley and taken to Uttoxeter, where Detective Inspector Frank Tucker charged him with Lainton's murder and he then made a written statement. He stated that he had married in 1949 and lived with his wife, Hilda, who was eight years younger than him, until 1951, when he was sentenced to five years in Dartmoor Prison on five counts of demanding money with menaces. This was not the first taste of prison that Cross had experienced and his previous history included stealing collecting boxes and cash in 1935 (Approved

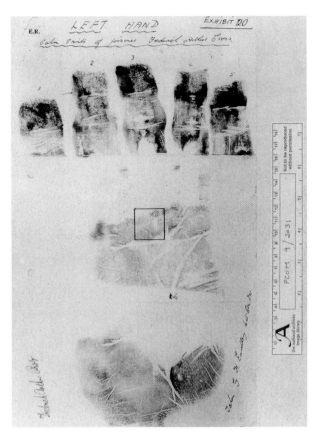

Frederick Arthur Cross's handprint, taken from the wing of the car at Birchen Bower Farm. (National Archives)

School), larceny of a motorcycle in London (three months), larceny of a wireless set (two months) and other lesser offences. He never knew his father and from an early age was put into a residential school but played truant so frequently that he was taken to court and sent to Padcroft Boys' Home until he reached the age of 16. There, he became depressed and attempted to commit suicide by swallowing aspirins. He worked in Hartley's jam factory prior to being called up into the army in August 1940, despite the fact that he was partially deaf, and served throughout the war in the RASC. On enlistment, he was adjudged to be in category A1, but on discharge his physical condition had sunk to C3. After discharge in 1946, he worked in the coalmines and had last been employed as a labourer for a firm in Stafford.

Released from Dartmoor Prison in 1955, having been given time off for good behaviour, he went back to his wife. They lived with their two children in a converted Nissen hut at Hillside, where he made the acquaintance of his next-door neighbour, George Ernest Greatholder, and his wife Ethel. Greatholder had been married for seven years and also had a criminal record, having had convictions for theft and blackmail, but the two neighbours appeared to get on with each other well enough and left for their respective jobs at about the same time each morning, Greatholder telling Cross that he worked for Tarmac. However, after a month or so, Cross began to get suspicious and one morning stayed behind and kept an eye on the Nissen hut, after his neighbour had supposedly gone to work. His suspicions proved justified as presently Greatholder returned and went into Cross's hut, where after biding his time for a few minutes, Cross found his wife and Greatholder in a compromising position.

It appeared that Greatholder had feigned going off to work every morning but sometimes returned to the hut to spend the day with Mrs Cross. Surprisingly, there was no major row after this incident and the two families continued to live as neighbours, but on New Year's Day 1955, Cross returned home from work to find his wife and children gone. A note said that she had left to live at an address in Wales with Greatholder, as his wife. Soon, Cross found out that his wife had gone leaving a mountain of debts, including several weeks' rent, and he had strong suspicions that she had been saving most of the housekeeping that he gave her in order to run away with her lover. Eager at first to clear all the debts as quickly as possible, he started to work seven days a week, but soon gave this up in despair. Although he appeared to have cared little for his wife before, Cross now fell into a deep depression and wrote to her, pleading with her to come back to him. There was no reply, so Cross bought the tin of rat poison to do away with himself, but found this act beyond him. Reading in the newspaper about a recent execution, he hit on the idea of committing a murder and then giving himself up, so that the law could take its course and solve his problem for him.

On 25 February, he went to the Coach & Horses, Pasturefields, Great Haywood, using his bicycle despite the wintry weather. He was an occasional visitor to the pub and on occasion he would play the piano there. The landlady, Lilian Lawson, saw him on that date and described him as a long-faced man of slight build and medium height. She had served him with ten Woodbines and a pint of bitter and they then fell into conversation, Cross suggesting that he should play the piano there on a regular basis, for which he would receive a modest payment. Mrs Lawson, thinking that the music would perhaps attract custom to her establishment, agreed and they were just on the point of shaking hands on the deal when in walked Donald Lainton, who ordered a gin and soda.

Cross stated that he had been brooding about his wife for some time and when Lainton came into the pub that day, he decided that the man, who he did not know, might well fit his plan exactly. He therefore struck up a conversation with Lainton and after having a drink together, and discussing where Lainton could get a meal, the two men left and the landlady saw them get into a car and drive away.

The former Coach & Horses public house at Pasturefields, where Donald Lainton met his nemesis. (Author's collection)

Cross now admitted that he had got Lainton to stop the car and had then attacked him with one half of a pair of scissors, which he said had belonged to Ethel Greatholder. In an unusual twist, the scissors turned out to have been given to Ethel by Cross's wife. Cross said, 'I struck him several blows on the head and chest. I just went berserk.' Afterwards, he said, he could remember nothing else until he found himself sitting alone in the car with Lainton's body in the back, having no knowledge of how it had got there. On 10 March, he had thrown the blade away in a field halfway up Blythe Bridge Bank, going towards Uttoxeter, where Detective Constable Eardley eventually found it, partly hidden under the snow which was still lying on the ground. A further search disclosed Lainton's chequebook, his driving license and other personal papers.

After Cross had finished making his statement, Detective Inspector Tucker asked him if he wished to apply for legal aid, to which Cross replied, 'I don't wish to apply for legal aid and I don't wish to be defended at all.' Later, in a court hearing held in the Council Chamber at Uttoxeter Town Hall, he was remanded in custody. At a later hearing, Cross still refused to be legally represented. Farmer William Stanley Crewe of Dowry Farm, Kingstone, said that he recognised the accused man as a person he had seen in the local post office on the day of the murder, trying to hire a taxi. The man was unsuccessful because of the weather and, eventually, he saw him getting a lift on a hay lorry. The driver of the lorry, Harry Bridge, said that he had accepted a 10s note from Cross to take him as far as the Coach & Horses at Hixon, where he saw him pick up a bicycle from behind a telephone box and ride off. It was his company's policy for their drivers not to give lifts – presumably the 10s note salved his conscience! Cross was eventually committed to the Summer Assizes at Stafford.

The accused man's insistence that he did not want to put up a defence and that he would plead guilty, in the express hope that he would be hanged, disturbed the authorities and the DPP file at the National Archives (which was originally closed until 2031 before it was released to the author under the Freedom of Information Act) states that it was decided by the Home Office to call in an outside psychiatrist to examine Cross. This was Dr J.L. Clegg of St Matthew's Hospital, Burntwood, near Lichfield, whose report stated that the accused was of a psychopathic personality from an early age, with a tendency to abnormal emotional reaction, to lack of judgement and foresight and to be unable to profit fully from experience. He was particular in stating that this did not amount to certifiable insanity, although in many persons so afflicted, he said, the resultant behaviour might reach such a degree from time to time. Clegg said that it was therefore impossible to express a definite opinion as to the state of Cross's mind at the actual moment of the attack upon Lainton and admitted that some degree of clouding of consciousness was usually accepted as part of the impulsive outbursts of aggression which were frequently shown by a psychopath. Cross was quite definite however about his intent to kill and that he intended the consequences of his actions, knowing that they were wrong. It is possible that a good defence counsel could have made something out of this rather ambivalent report, but in the event, Cross insisted that he wanted no representation at the trial and so any chance that he might have been saved was thus lost.

The trial began before Mr Justice Gorman on Tuesday 5 July 1955, Cross appearing in an open-necked shirt and a light-coloured mackintosh. It soon became clear that he was very hard of hearing and it was arranged that the prison officer, who had accompanied him into the dock, would repeat the proceedings as they went along. Mr Justice Gorman had, of course, already been informed that Cross did not have legal representation and his first words to the accused man were on this matter. 'I asked that you be informed that if you required legal representation, then I would be happy to arrange it for you,' he told Cross. 'But I understand that you do not require such assistance.' Leaning forward, he said slowly and in a loud voice, 'Is that right?'

The prison officer repeated the judge's words to Cross, who muttered something that the judge heard. 'I understand from what you have just said that you do not want it,' he said. Cross replied, 'No. I want to plead guilty.'

At these words, there was a considerable commotion in the public gallery, which the judge silenced with a scowl and a wave of his hand. Anxious that the accused man should fully understand his position, the judge went on, 'You do understand that if you plead guilty to this charge, I shall have no alternative but to pass sentence? Do you fully understand that?' Once again, after having the words repeated to him, Cross replied in the affirmative.

The Clerk of the Assizes, Mr J. Tumim, then said to Cross, 'You stand convicted on your own confession of wilful murder. Have you anything to say why the court should not now give you judgement to die according to law?' Cross replied 'Yes sir,' but said nothing further.

Plainly disturbed by these events, Mr Justice Gorman paused while the square of black silk was placed on his head and then pronounced sentence of death. The whole trial had taken no more than eight minutes from start to finish and must have been one of the shortest murder trials on record.

While awaiting execution, Cross wrote to his mother:

Well mum, I wish I never come out of Dartmoor and I thought I had something to come home to till I found out all Hilda had been doing while I was away. It was a shock when I found her gone. I just could not believe it of her and I was simply struck down by it, so I did what I did so as to be sure they would do the same to me and I can only ask your forgiveness for the shame I have given our family. Fondest love,

Your loving son
Fred

He also wrote a similar letter to his sister, Mrs Rose Howes, telling her that he was being allowed a ration of twenty cigarettes a day. In all this, Cross does not seem to have expressed any regret about his victim, the unsuspecting and innocent Donald Lainton. One week before the execution, a letter, signed by both his mother and his mother-in-law, was sent to the Queen, asking her to intercede, and as usual this was forwarded to the Home Secretary, who declined to take any action.

On Tuesday 26 July 1955, Albert Pierrepoint and Harry Allen, both publicans in their normal occupation, granted Frederick Arthur Cross's wish with a drop of 6ft 8in, while a crowd of about eighty people, mostly women and children, gathered outside Birmingham Prison. Unusually, the police were present in some force, as if awaiting some form of demonstration, but this did not happen. The usual time for execution was 9 a.m. and there were hushed conversations among the crowd as the clock hands reached 9.37 a.m. without any indication that the execution had taken place. Suddenly, there was a movement as two prison warders brought out the noticeboard containing the official notice and, still muttering about the unexplained delay, the crowd slowly drifted away.

Over the next fourteen days there were to be two more executions at the prison, but the execution of Arthur Cross was to be the last performed by Albert Pierrepoint at Birmingham. At no time did Cross express any remorse or sympathy for his victim.

12

DEATH ON THE CHASE

Cannock Chase, 1967

On the early afternoon of 8 September 1965, 6-year-old Margaret Reynolds, a month short of her seventh birthday, left her home in Clifton Road, Aston, a suburb of Birmingham, to return to school, a journey from which she never returned. When she did not arrive home at the usual time, her mother began to get anxious and informed the local police. The forces of the law are always concerned when a child goes missing, although in the early stages it is always likely that the child will turn up, having been distracted by one thing or another, but nightfall came and young Margaret had not appeared, nor had she returned by the following morning, by which time her parents were distraught.

Over the next two months, a team of police numbering 150 went from house to house, patiently asking each inhabitant whether they had seen any trace of the young girl, but the answer was always the same. It seemed that Margaret had disappeared into thin air and the more experienced of the police searchers knew in their hearts that this almost certainly meant that the little girl had been abducted and killed. More than 25,000 people were interviewed, canals and standing waters were painstakingly dragged and derelict buildings gone through, but in the end, the search wound down, although some officers still continued to sift through the dribble of information that came in from the public, most of it well-meaning but useless.

Suddenly, the search came to life again, when on 30 December 1965, a second girl, 5-year-old Diane Joy Tift, went missing while out playing near her home in Walsall. She was last seen alive at around 2 p.m., carrying a small pink plastic handbag, when she left her grandmother's house in Chapel Street, Bloxwich, to go to her home at 2 Hollemeadow Avenue. A house-to-house search yielded no information about the missing girl and by 1 January 1966, more than 500 officers were involved in the search, including Regional Crime Squads from Wolverhampton, Birmingham and Stoke-on-Trent.

Detective Superintendent Cyril Gold, a small, dapper man, accompanied by his Sergeant, Eric Bailey, was called in from Scotland Yard's Murder Squad to head the investigation and assist Chief Superintendent Harry Bailey, the head of Staffordshire County CID. Once again, teams of divers examined streams and pools, while lines of policemen and volunteers went through waist-high fern and scrub, searching for any clue that might lead to the discovery of the two girls. Disused quarries and mine workings were searched meticulously and every possible place where a young child's body might have been hidden was examined, but all to no avail. It was to be a man out hunting for rabbits on Cannock Chase, a vast area of forest and heath land stretching from a few miles north of Birmingham almost to Stafford, who stumbled on Diane Tift's body on 12 January, half concealed by undergrowth on the edge of a ditch alongside a farmer's field. The Chase was the haunt of walkers, hunters and, of course, lovers, but for all that remained remote and lonely. The girl's body lay in a waterlogged ditch near Pottal Pool, at a place known as Mansty Gully, half a mile from the A34 near the village of Huntington, just north of Cannock. While the police were carrying out the gruesome task of lifting Diane's remains from the tangle of foliage that had partly concealed it from sight, they discovered a second set of remains underneath. Little was left of the second body, apart from the skeleton and a child's shoe, but the police felt that it was safe to assume that this was the body of the missing Margaret Reynolds. There was too little of her left for the forensic scientists to even guess as to how she had met her death, but Diane Tift had been suffocated by someone pulling her pixie hood over her face and pressing hard on her mouth and nose. At her post-mortem, forensic pathologists were assisted by the fact that icy weather over the past two weeks had helped to preserve the body and there was still evidence of a sexual attack on the 5-year-old child.

Over the next five months, the double murder enquiry ground on painstakingly, every member of the police and forensic personnel working on the case determined that they would bring the callous killer to justice. House-to-house enquiries were made with no result, although the police did have one moment of hope when they discovered that the man who had found the bodies at Mansty Gully had a record of violence, but he was soon shown to be unconnected with the killings. There were also reports in the area of a man calling himself 'Uncle Len,' who had tried to entice young girls into his motorcar and the police let it be known that they were seeking this man, 'To eliminate him from police enquiries.'

Other unsolved crimes were re-examined and the police concentrated especially on the case of 9-year-old Julia Taylor, who, on 1 December 1964, had been lured into a car in the Bloxwich area by a man who told her that he was a friend of her mother and would take her to collect some Christmas presents. Instead, he drove her to a quiet place and subjected her to a sexual attack and then strangled her, throwing her out of the car, leaving her for dead. In the early evening, the young girl recovered consciousness in a wayside ditch, soaked through by the falling rain and must surely have died there from exposure if she had not been spotted by a passing cyclist.

The ditch at Mansty Gully, which concealed two bodies. (Author's collection)

She could remember little of her ordeal, only that the car into which she had been enticed was painted in two colours and a witness who had seen her get into the vehicle thought that it might have been a Vauxhall Cresta, with a spotlight mounted on the driver's side front door. This seemingly important clue at first came to nothing and the mystery of the attack was never formally solved, but information of this nature continued to build up in the Incident Room at Cannock police station. With computers being very much in their infancy, this information was stored in filing cabinets and boxes, with no cross-reference system to speak of, and by June 1967 the trail was, to all intents and purposes, cold. In the late 1970s, ten years on, this lack of a proper system was also to severely hamper the hunt for the Yorkshire Ripper.

No further clues of any substance appeared, and at length, Superintendent Gold and Detective Sergeant Bailey returned to Scotland Yard, leaving the ongoing investigation in the hands of the local men.

On 19 August 1967, a group of young children were playing in Camden Street, Walsall, a narrow road of terraced houses, and among them was 7-year-old Christine Darby. A pretty little girl, always smiling, she sported dark hair with a fringe and was dressed in dark blue jeans, a white T-shirt and black plimsolls. She was with her 8-year-old friend Nicholas Baldry and another boy, Alwyn Isaacs, when at about 2.30 p.m. a car drew up alongside the group and the driver wound down his window and spoke to them. 'Do you know the way to Caldmoor Green?' The man spoke with a local accent and pronounced the name of the district 'Carmer,' as the locals did. The children knew the area well and described how the man could get there, but he seemed unable to understand their instructions and asked Christine if she would get into the car and show him the way, promising that he would bring her back to her friends afterwards.

The child, forgetting the instructions of her mother never to talk to strangers, obligingly got into the car, which reversed and drove off, leaving Diane's young friends puzzled. They knew very well where Caldmoor Green lay and the car had driven off in the opposite direction. Having themselves many times been warned by anxious parents that they should on no account talk to strangers or get into strange motorcars, they ran off to raise the alarm.

Arriving at Christine's house, they shouted out their news to her mother, Mrs Lilian Darby, who immediately rushed to inform the police. Although the main search for the other two missing girls had run down, the police still had a plan up their sleeves in case of another abduction, which involved the closure of all the main roads leading towards Cannock Chase and this plan was immediately put into action. Of the driver, and his light-coloured car, however, there was no sign. Nicholas Baldry described the man as being aged between 35 and 40 (an amazing piece of deduction from an 8-year-old); thin, clean-shaven with dark brown hair, and driving an Austin Cambridge or Morris Oxford saloon. The young lad had been shown a series of colour photographs of cars, from which he had picked the most likely model. Several witnesses came forward with stories of a grey-coloured Morris Oxford saloon that had been seen outside a local school during the past two weeks, but no one had thought to take down the number. Detective Chief Superintendent Harry Bailey, still the local man in charge of the case, was certain that the Cannock Chase killer had struck again.

The next day, Bailey's men were out searching the Cannock Chase area, a superhuman task as the Chase spread out over some ninety square miles, much of it planted with thick groves of fir trees, with bracken often up to shoulder height. All the main roads leading to the Chase were watched by uniformed police officers and 24,000 handouts were printed and given out to the public. These bore a picture of Christine Darby and the question, 'Were you on Cannock Chase on Saturday 19 August after 2.30 p.m.?'

People responded in their hundreds to this and other requests by the police in the press and many were the outwardly respectable men who had been 'clocked' by someone parked up in the lonely glades of Cannock Chase with women who were most definitely not their wives! The police treated these incidents with understanding and tact and were probably responsible for saving many a marriage that summer.

Camden Street, Walsall, where Christine Darby was abducted. (Author's collection)

People throughout the Midlands and Staffordshire were asked to check parks and moorland areas and there was an appeal for news of any man who had suddenly left his home address or his workplace. The Assistant Chief Constable (Crime) in the West Midlands, Gerald Baumber, told the press that he thought that someone was deliberately shielding the killer and reminded everyone that it was their public duty to come forward with any information that they had. This statement was to prove remarkably prescient in view of later events. Mansty Gully was once more attracting more attention than the police would have liked, as the summer weather brought out hundreds of rubbernecking motorists. They were rewarded by having their vehicles thoroughly searched and their names taken.

The first breakthrough came on Sunday 20 August, by which time over 750 people were engaged in the search for Christine Darby, including 200 soldiers of the Mercian Brigade from Whittington Barracks at Lichfield and fifty airmen from 16 MU, the maintenance unit at Stafford. Half the searchers were combing dense undergrowth for twenty yards on each side of the A34, while the rest were told to search 'in depth' with the assistance of twenty-five police dogs, to clear the area round three gravel pits.

Among them was PC Arthur Ellis of the mounted section, who was riding in an extended line with his colleagues, eastwards from Pottal Pool crossroads on the A34 trunk road. It was 11.15 a.m. and he was about half a mile from the crossroads when he caught sight of a piece of cloth caught on the branch of a fallen tree. Dismounting, he inspected the piece and found it to be a pair of child's knickers. From the look of them, they had not been there long.

Christine's grandmother collapsed in floods of tears when they were shown to her. They had definitely belonged to her granddaughter, for she recognised a repair that she had made herself. The police now concentrated their search in the Pottal Pool area and eventually more than fourteen miles of binder twine was used to delineate the lanes which were then methodically examined for any signs of the missing girl.

On 22 August, the *Staffordshire Sentinel* reported in banner headlines that a black plimsoll, much like the ones that Christine Darby had been wearing, had been found by a woodman, about two and a half miles away from the spot where her underclothing had been found. The shoe was the same size and colour, the knot was similar to the one that Christine tied and her grandmother, Henrietta Darby, once again had no difficulty in identifying it as belonging to her granddaughter. Some hours later, around 5 p.m., the searchers were nearing a part of the forest known as 'Plantation 110.' They had been advancing slowly in an extended line for a good nine hours, probing through the scrub and fern that made their task even more difficult, but were still willing to carry on until the light failed. Forty-five minutes later, when most of the men were definitely thinking that maybe they had done their fair share for the day, Private Michael Blundred shouted for the line to halt. Covered by ferns that had been spread over her, lay the body of Christine Darby.

The rule in a murder enquiry is that, until proved otherwise, a murder is deemed to have taken place where the body is found. This meant that although the abduction had taken place inside another police authority boundary, the main responsibility now fell on the Staffordshire police and it was Chief Constable Arthur M. Rees who had to make the decision as to whether or not to call in Scotland Yard. He did not hesitate and within hours, Detective Superintendent Ian Forbes, a bluff Scot, with his sergeant, Tom Parry, was descending from the London train at Stafford station, to be greeted by Chief Superintendent Harry Baily.

Straight away, the men from Scotland Yard were driven to Cannock Chase, where the body of Christine Darby lay on a ridge between two furrows, arms and legs akimbo, naked from the waist down. With the light beginning to fail, a decision was made to cover the body and leave it there under police guard until the morning, when Professor Alan Usher, the Home Office pathologist from Sheffield, could make his initial examination. Until then, it remained protected by a 9ft-sq. white tent.

The inquest opened on Wednesday afternoon, before the Stafford coroner, Mr K.T. Braine-Hartnell, at Stafford General Infirmary, the coroner reminding those present of the inquest held eighteen months ago on Margaret Reynolds and Diane Tift. 'Christine,' he said, 'came from much the same area and

Plantation 110, Cannock Chase, where Christine Darby's body was discovered. (Author's collection)

was abducted in more or less the same manner as the other two girls. The circumstances of her killing were also strikingly similar to the others.' Adjourning the inquest until 12 December, so that the police could continue their enquiries, he expressed sympathy for the family and friends of the three dead girls.

Meanwhile, the police involvement was rapidly increasing and there were now two murder incident rooms, one at Walsall and the other at Cannock police HQ. In a newsworthy move, a closed-circuit television link was set up between the two incident rooms, the first time this had been attempted in Britain. Row after row of metal filing boxes appeared and were rapidly filled as the investigation moved on. Towards the end of the investigation, at Cannock alone, these were to number over three-dozen filing cabinets, and a similar number of card index drawers. A huge map of Cannock Chase was fixed to one wall, covered in button pins, each one a sighting of a motor vehicle on the Chase.

A formidable team was now assembled under Detective Superintendent Ian Forbes, including Arthur Rees, Chief Constable of Staffordshire, assisted by Chief Superintendent Harry Bailey, head of Staffordshire CID, Mr Gerald Baumber, Assistant Chief Constable (Crime) West Midlands Police, Professor Alan Usher, the Sheffield pathologist, and the newly arrived identikit expert from Scotland Yard, Detective Sergeant Talbot.

Alan Usher had now completed his examination of Christine Darby and reported that she had been sexually assaulted and asphyxiated, probably within twenty-four hours of being abducted. Further examination of Plantation 110 revealed car tracks running approximately 150 yards along a bridleway and ending close to where the body had been discovered. The car had been driven in and then reversed back up to the roadway again. This set off another bout of publicity, both in the newspapers and on television, asking for everyone who had been in a car on the Chase that day to come forward, which led to over 600 cars and their drivers being eliminated from the investigation. In the end, they were left with only one, a Volkswagen Beetle.

At first, repeated requests for the owner to come forward failed, but finally, a Mr Victor Whitehouse contacted the police, full of apologies because the police description of where his car was supposed to have been seen was wrong and so he had ignored the requests. Now, it seemed that he could be an important witness, as he was a keen fan of the open air and visited the Chase on most days, walking with his dog. He was able to describe a man who had been standing beside a greyish Austin A60 that had been backed up into the trees. Several others remembered this car and between them were able to give the police an identikit picture that was then circulated freely in the media, including television. It was the first time that an identikit had been published in colour, thanks to an artist from the *Birmingham Mail*, who volunteered to perform this task. It is important to remember that the identikit picture is not a photograph, but rather a collection of facial features; in this case, a slightly creased forehead, prominent cheekbones, a bulbous nose and teeth that showed slightly through the lips. It would be found later that although the identikit picture in its totality did not look much like the accused man, the different parts of the picture matched very well.

Altogether, as the investigation wore on, 25,000 car owners were eliminated from the enquiry and owners of grey Austin A55s and A60s who had left the country were traced throughout Europe and as far away as Africa and the Far East, but with no result. A businessman in Walsall offered to place £1,000 into a special 'reward' fund being raised by the Mayor, who promptly called a press conference to announce that the money would go to anyone who, in the opinion of the Chief Constable of Staffordshire, supplied information leading to the conviction of the killer. Visitors to Cannock Chase over the Easter holiday were asked to be on the lookout for Christine's missing plimsoll and to try to recall if they had seen anyone acting suspiciously the previous weekend, meanwhile uniformed police officers manned all entrances to the Chase and distributed thousands of leaflets appealing for information. One man wrote to Detective Superintendent Bailey that the police might be dealing with a case of witchcraft and warned that another child could be at risk in the next ten days. This and many other similar letters were to be expected in any notorious murder case, but they all still had to be considered and time wasted on them. Many cranks wrote, usually anonymously, confessing to the crimes; but all the information that they had could have been gleaned from the newspapers and television programmes.

Early on Thursday 31 August, Forbes travelled to Sheffield to discuss the case with Professor Usher and to receive the pathologist's full report, before driving to attend the funeral of Christine Darby, which took place at the Pentecostal Chapel in Walsall. Officers in plain clothes mingled with the mourners, scanning the faces of those present, looking for the identikit killer, but they were disappointed.

Despite all the frenzied publicity and the activity of hundreds of police personnel, the weeks went by without any further clue coming to light and in August 1968 Forbes and his sergeant returned to London, bitterly disappointed at the outcome and desperate for some leave after their exertions of the past year. Within a month, much refreshed, they were back on the job and before many weeks had passed, the breakthrough for which they had been hoping arrived at last.

On the evening on 4 November 1968, a 10-year-old girl, Margaret Aulton, was finishing off a bonfire, ready for Guy Fawkes Night the following day. As she placed pieces of wood on a piece of spare ground in Bridgeman Street, Walsall, a man approached, smartly dressed and wearing a grey suit, and asked her if she would like some fireworks. Forgetting what her mother had often told her about talking to strangers, she scrambled into the man's car but, when she could not see any of the promised fireworks, she wriggled out again, despite the man catching hold of her arm. A young married woman, Wendy Lane, had seen the incident and she was later able to identify the car as a green and white Ford Corsair and the number plate, 429 LOP, which she had made a mental note of at the time. The police soon realised that Mrs Lane had made a mistake in either the numbers or the letters and by a process of juggling, found that it was in fact registration 492 LOP that belonged to a green and cream Ford Corsair. It turned out that this was the only green and cream Corsair with the registration LOP and it belonged to 39-year-old engineer Raymond Leslie Morris, who lived in a block of high-rise council flats at 20 Regent House, Green Lane, Walsall.

After serving as an apprentice to a pattern maker, Morris had completed his two year's National Service and had later progressed to works foreman at L.J. Taylor Ltd, of Oldbury. He was easy to find as he was living with his second wife, Carol (his first wife had divorced him because of his violent behaviour), in a block of flats that overlooked Walsall police station!

The police were struck by the man's resemblance to the identikit picture, whose circulation was now widespread, and they were even more convinced that they had at last got their man when investigations revealed that this man had also previously owned a slate-grey Austin Cambridge A55. The news that Morris had also owned a two-tone Vauxhall Cresta with a spotlight on the driver's door put the last piece of the jigsaw in place.

It then turned out that Raymond Morris had been involved with the police before. During October 1966 he was suspected of taking indecent photographs of young schoolgirls, although the case had not been proceeded with due to lack of evidence. It was clear from the contents of the flat, however, that Morris was very much into photography and as the registered owner of a grey Austin Cambridge motorcar, he had been among the many men interviewed by the Walsall police after Christine's killing and he was seen on 5 September, just seventeen days after the murder. He told the police that he had left work just after 1 p.m. on Saturday 19 August and arrived home before 2 p.m., thereafter going out shopping with his wife. He also claimed that his way home took him nowhere near Camden Street. Carole Morris happily backed up his story and so, for the time being, the police turned their attention to other suspects.

After the Margaret Aulton episode, Morris was put in a police line-up but Mrs Lane failed to pick him out. She had, however, given quite a detailed description of the man she had seen, which included that he had been wearing a silver-coloured watch with a bracelet on it. On 15 November 1968, the police were ready to move. Morris was arrested in his green and cream Corsair at 7 a.m., as he was on his way to work, and was taken to Stafford police station. When Inspector Molloy told him that he was being

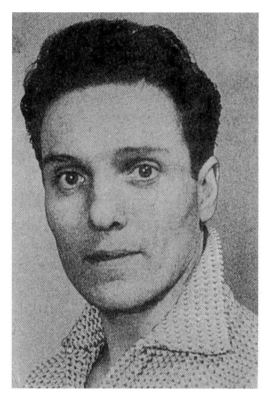

Raymond Leslie Morris. (Author's collection)

Regent House, where Raymond Leslie Morris lived at no. 20, overlooking Walsall police station. (Author's collection)

Above: *Walsall police station was just 80 yards from the killer's house in 1967.* (Author's collection)

Right: *The identikit picture of Raymond Leslie Morris.* (Author's collection)

detained in connection with the murder of Christine Darby, he blanched and stuttered, 'Oh God, is it the wife?' Despite this, he still strenuously denied that he had had anything to do with Christine's death but this time, when asked to go on an identification parade, Morris declined. After several times refusing the parade, Forbes worked a ruse that he had no doubt used before and, waiting till Morris was alone in the exercise yard, he allowed Victor Whitehouse, the man who had seen him on Cannock Chase, to enter the yard and get a close look at him. Whitehouse identified his man with barely a moment's hesitation.

The police had suspected all along that Carol Morris had been lying to protect her husband and she was brought into Hednesford police station and questioned about her husband's movements. Afterwards, she was taken back to her flat, which was searched from top to bottom. This time, a large number of pornographic photographs were found, the production of which seemed to come as a shock to Morris's 25-year-old wife. Within hours, she had confessed that on the day that Christine was murdered, her husband had not arrived home from work until at least 4.30 p.m., three hours after the time he had previously stated. This information was enough to charge Morris with murder and after a further long interview, during which he affected a show of indifference to whatever was going to happen to him, he was sent to Winson Green Prison to await his first appearance in court. In common with normal practice, Morris was strip-searched on arrival at the prison and somewhat to their surprise, the prison officers found strapped to his ankle a wristwatch on a metal bracelet, exactly as the one Mrs Lane had described. Morris was able to give no cogent reason as to why the watch was there. The answer soon came. During the search of Morris's flat, the officers had found a box of photographic paper marked, 'Only to be opened in a darkened room.' The local police photographer happily obliged and the box was opened; inside were dozens of photographs, mostly pornographic and in several of them was a man, his face obscured, but on his wrist could clearly be seen the watch.

Ten days after her husband's arrest, Carol Morris made a second statement, confirming her amended story that Morris had been late home on the day of the murder. His works time card showed that he had clocked off just after 1 p.m. and to excuse his lateness coming home, he had told his wife that he had stayed behind, talking to his boss. They then went to the Marks & Spencer store in Walsall, to buy some cakes that her mother had particularly asked her to get. The reason why she had supported her husband's original story was that she could not imagine for one instant that he could be guilty of such a crime and therefore thought that it would not matter if she just went along with what he said. Something, possibly fright, prevented her from questioning her husband after the police had gone.

At the Shire Hall, Stafford, the trial opened on 10 February 1969, when Raymond Leslie Morris pleaded 'Not Guilty' to a charge of murdering

Christine Darby; and 'Not Guilty' to a charge of attempted abduction in the case of Margaret Aulton, but 'Guilty' to indecently assaulting the 5-year-old child pictured in the photographs found in his flat. Unprecedented public interest meant that queues of over a hundred formed each day for seats in the public gallery. On the second day, Nicholas Baldry, now 9 years old, struggled to recall the events of almost fifteen months ago and although he remembered Christine Darby getting into a car, he had forgotten about the pronunciation of 'Carmer' Green. Victor Whitehouse stood firm in his identification of the man he had seen with his car on the Chase, as did another witness, Mrs Mary Rawlings, who had seen Morris as she was walking her dog. The following day, the public gallery was packed for what everyone felt would be the defining moment of the trial – it was the turn of Carol Morris to give evidence. She looked pale and had lost weight since her husband had first been arrested; the more keen-eyed of those in the courtroom would have noticed that there was no wedding or engagement ring on her left hand. She studiously avoided her husband's gaze as she confirmed that she had lied about the time he came home from work on 19 August 1967 and that he invariably came home on a route that took him near Camden Street and Caldmore Green. She was questioned closely about her previous support for her husband's statements and finally had to admit that she had done so because 'I knew that what I was saying was untrue, but I couldn't believe it.' Morris's mother and father-in-law were positive that he and Carol had arrived at their house just as the football results on the television were being given, which had fixed the time in their minds. For a change, the judge revealed himself to be a man of the world, remarking that anyone who knew anything about anything knew that the football results always came on at five o'clock!

At length, the prosecution turned its attention to the attempted abduction at Bridgeman Street. Young Margaret Aulton had not been able to identify Morris and so attention was directed at Wendy Lane, who had mistakenly given the police the wrong car registration number. She quickly admitted that she had made a mistake with the numbers, but defended herself by pointing out that the numbers were the correct ones, although not in the right order. The seventy-sixth and penultimate prosecution witness was Chief Superintendent Forbes, followed finally by Chief Inspector Pat Molloy. The desperation of defence counsel was well illustrated when he accused Molloy of striking Morris three times at Stafford police station, an accusation that the policeman stoutly denied.

Raymond Morris now went into the witness box and in a quiet voice stuck to his original story about the time he had arrived home on the day of Christine Darby's murder and the route he had taken. He complained that his wife had originally been telling the truth but now, for some reason he could not comprehend, she was lying about him. All the police evidence, according to him, was made up and was a complete fabrication. Suddenly, there was a commotion in the courtroom as a young teenage girl in the public gallery shouted, 'That's him. That's the man that did it to me' and was led away, crying, by the ushers. The people in court were not to know that this was Julia Taylor, the young girl who had been abducted at Bloxwich just before Christmas 1964 and who had been left for dead in the ditch. Julia had presumably been brought to the Shire Hall by her parents, but whether the prosecution knew this, or were expecting her to cry out, is not known.

The examination proceeded with the production of the pornographic photographs found at the flat. Morris had no explanation for these, or for the poses that the girl, who was actually his wife's niece, had taken up. When it was suggested that one pose was exactly like the position of Christine Darby when she met her death, he affected not to understand the question.

When the matter of the wristwatch, found at Winson Green Prison, was put to him, he replied that he had just 'kept it on', a reply that the judge made it quite clear that he found unacceptable. Morris also denied that he had ever said, 'Oh God. Was it the wife?' when he was arrested by Inspector Molloy and insisted that the policeman had lied in his evidence about that incident. He also claimed that Molloy had assaulted him during the arrest, a charge that Molloy hotly denied. By the end of his ordeal in the witness box, Raymond Green had been interrogated for over six hours, spread over two days. The jury of nine men and three women had no trouble in finding him guilty on all counts and he was given sentences of life imprisonment, three years and one year, all to run concurrently. Subsequently, an appeal failed.

Nothing was ever proved against Raymond Morris for the deaths of Diane Tift and Margaret Reynolds and he was never charged with their deaths. These crimes remain unsolved although the police were satisfied these crimes had been resolved once Morris was safely behind bars. Morris's Austin Cambridge was later bought by a car dealer, who burned it on his garage forecourt, watched by a large crowd.

It later came to light that an amazing incident in 1965 might have solved two murders and prevented a third. After the Mansty Gully killings, Raymond Morris's brother walked into Cannock police station of his own accord and made a statement, naming Raymond Morris as the killer! He described his brother as a man of abnormal sexual appetites, cold and cruel and, in his opinion, quite capable of committing the Mansty Gully murders. Of course, the brother could not produce any evidence to back up his statement and it is highly likely that the police dealing with him at the time decided that he was just one more of the 'nutters' who pestered them in such cases. In the event, his statement was marked 'No Further Action' and was filed away without proper indexing, resulting in it becoming lost in the system until it was too late to affect the outcome. If Agatha Christie had included such a subplot in one of her books, it would have been regarded as being over the top!

Over thirty years later, in 2001, newspapers reported that Morris, now in Wymott Prison, Preston, was attempting to appeal his sentence on the basis that he was convicted on dubious circumstantial evidence, but retired (and promoted) Chief Superintendent Pat Molloy reportedly said that he had no doubt that Morris was rightly convicted. 'The Cannock Chase murders and abductions of little girls was going on for four years and involved a huge operation. It stopped dead after Morris's arrest and there have been no more since.' He continued, 'I would describe him as cold, cruel, lustful and just plain wicked.'

The three boxes of MEPO files at the National Archive are closed until 2063 and despite the author's request for production under the Freedom of Information Act, permission for them to be opened was flatly denied. The same applies to the ASSI files and it seems that the photographs and information contained therein are too dreadful for the public gaze. Despite having written confirmation that the ASSI files were held at Kew, but that they would not be produced under the Freedom of Information Act, when the author searched for them again at a later stage of his research, the system refused even to acknowledge their existence.

Raymond Leslie Morris is unlikely to leave prison alive.

BIBLIOGRAPHY

BOOKS

Bedford, Paul, *Gaskin*, Cromwell Press, 2006

Bell, David, *Murder Casebook*, Countryside Books, 1996

Bell, David, *Staffordshire & Black Country Murder Casebook*, Countryside Books, 1996

Birmingham City Archives, MS 1815/11

Cox, David J. & Pearson Michael, *Foul Deeds & Suspicious Deaths around the Black Country*, Wharncliffe Books, 2006

Ellis, John, *Diary of a Hangman*, Forum Press, 1996

Fletcher, George, *The Life & Career of Dr William Palmer*, T. Fisher Unwin Ltd, 1925

Forbes, Ian, *Squad Man*, W.H. Allen, 1973

Godwin John, *The Murder of Christina Collins*

Jamieson, W.M, *Murder,Myths & Monuments of North Staffordshire*, Westmid, 1979

Knott, G.H. (ed.), *Trial of William Palmer*, Notable English Trials Series, Hodge & Co., 1912

Lewis, Dave, *The Rugeley Poisoner – A Biography*, Artloaf, 2003

Molloy, Pat, *The Cannock Chase Murders*, Gomer Press, 1988

Pierrepoint, Albert. *Executioner:Pierrepoint*. Harrap. 1974

Van Der Elst, *On The Gallows*, Doge Press, 1937

Woolaston, Thomas, *Police Experiences*, Bates, 1884. Reprinted by Berkswich History Society, Stafford, 2007

Illustrated Life & Career of Wm. Palmer of Rugeley, Ward & Lock, 1856

NEWSPAPERS

Birmingham Mail
Birmingham Post & Mail
Daily Express
Illustrated London News
Liverpool Echo
News of the World
Staffordshire Advertiser
Staffordshire Newsletter
Staffordshire Sentinel
The Star
The Times
Wolverhampton Express & Star

FILES FROM THE NATIONAL ARCHIVES, KEW

P.R.O. TS11/430 – 434
TS 25/922 & 927
CRIM. 4/551
P.R.O. PCOM 8/61
P.R.O. HO 144/1694/411804 *
PCOM 8/27
P.R.O. ASSI 6/76/9
HO 144/23283 *
PCOM 9/1151 *
P.R.O. ASSI 6/78/15
HO 45/23932 & 3
PCOM 9/1239 *
P.R.O. ASSI 89/4 *
ASSI 6/85 *^
P.COM 9/1493 *
P.R.O. ASSI 6/109
ASSI 89/25 *
DPP 2/2416 *^
PCOM 9/2031
ASSI 6/527, 528 & 529 ++ (closed until 2063)

* *indicates those P.R.O. files which were closed until released at the request of the author under the Freedom of Information Act 2000.*
*^ *indicates that although the file was released, items were missing from it, usually photographs.*
++ *indicates that requisition for the file under the Freedom of Information Act 2000 was refused entirely.*

INDEX